MY
BROTHER'S
KEEPER

Eli Ginzberg

Transaction Publishers
New Brunswick (U.S.A.) and London (U.K.)

Library of Congress Catalog Number: 88-36523
ISBN: 0–88738–291–6
Printed in the United States of America

Library of Congress Cataloging-in-Publication Data

Ginzberg, Eli, 1911–
    My brother's keeper / Eli Ginzberg.

        p.   cm.
    Bibliography: p.
    Includes index.
    ISBN 0-88738-291-6
    1. Ginzberg, Eli, 1911–   . 2. Jews — United States — Biography.
3. Economists — United States — Biography. I. Title.
E184.J5G466   1989
973′.04924024 — dc19   88-36523
    [B]   CIP

To the memory of
Frank I. Schechter
and in celebration of
four generations of friendship between the Schechter
and the Ginzberg families

Contents

Acknowledgments

After I had completed a draft of the manuscript I benefited from the advice of my daughter, Abigail, and four friends who read it: Professor Moses Abramovitz of Stanford University; Professor Irving Louis Horowitz, President of Transaction Publishers, Rutgers University; Mrs. Miriam Ostow, Conservation of Human Resources, Columbia University; and Professor Yosef Hayim Yerushalmi of Columbia University. The advice that I received from them helped me to improve the manuscript, but they are absolved of all responsibility for the shortcomings that remain.

My longtime associate, Mrs. Anna B. Dutka, took on the arduous task of checking all of the details involving names, dates, and numbers, for which I am greatly in her debt.

Mrs. Sylvia Leef and Ms. Shoshana Vasheetz processed the successive drafts, from transcribing my difficult hand to preparing the final copy for the printer, for which I thank them.

Acknowledgments

1

Themes and Directions

This book assesses major transformations in the lives and institutions of American Jews in the twentieth century, using as the point of departure my personal involvement in some, and my ongoing study of other of these transformations. To claim that this effort is an exercise in historical scholarship would be pretentious, but it would also be wrong to view it solely as a foray into autobiographical writing. It is a mixture of the two.

I have sought to illuminate selective aspects of the transformations that American Jews have experienced during this century in the dominant areas of their lives—as individuals in search of a better future; in their attitudes and behavior toward Jewish communal activities, in particular the synagogue, philanthropy, and Jewish education; their changing relations to their fellow citizens; and their involvement with, and support for Jews in other countries, particularly those in Israel.

But I claim some special advantages that have helped me in developing this personal retrospective. The first relates to the length of my perspective: as a seventy-seven-year-old, I have lived much longer than most of my compatriots and co-religionists. Age is surely no guarantee of understanding, and even less of wisdom, but if perspective is needed, then age is an advantage. As will become clear in the next chapter, I started with a major assist: my father helped me to understand and interpret the paths and bypaths of two millennia of Jewish experience in the Diaspora. My discipline, economics, and a specialty in human resources provided me with useful tools. And I have been not only an observer but an active participant in some of the transformations that comprise the core of this account. What is more, I have been forced in developing this retrospective to come to terms with—or at least to become aware of—the multiplicity of forces that have pulled me in different directions with respect to my own "Jewishness" in the realms of both ideas and behavior.

I can remember the noise, crowding, and poverty that characterized the lower East Side of New York City in the mid-1920s when I was an ambulatory patient at the old Beth Israel Hospital. There are still a great many Jewish families in the lower income brackets, but in the mid-1920s the proportion was much larger. At that time only a relatively small number of Jews were in the higher income brackets. In the 1930s Father Coughlin attracted an ever larger radio audience whose listeners he harangued with scurrilous attacks on the Jews, their power, and their nefarious behavior. He was well advanced in making anti-Semitism a potent force in the political arena when his ecclesiastical superiors silenced him. For those of us oldsters who remember Father Coughlin and others of his ilk, it is hard to buy into the increasingly fashionable theory of contemporary analysts of the Jewish scene in the United States, which holds that political anti-Semitism is a scourge that has been permanently eliminated. If all continues to go well that may indeed turn out to be the correct forecast. But history is a warning that things seldom continue to turn out well.

At the outbreak of World War II, Eastern Europe was the heartbeat of the Diaspora, surely when measured in terms of number of Jews who lived Jewish lives and who were loyal to their tradition. At the end of the war, 6 million of these Eastern European Jews had been exterminated and there remained nothing more than a few artifacts from the creative culture of more than half a millennium.

The slaughter of the innocents was camouflaged by the still greater slaughter that was occurring on both the Eastern and the Western fronts, a camouflage aided and abetted by the press and by all the political leaders of the West, from President Franklin D. Roosevelt to Pope Pius XII. But the silence of the Christian leadership is less surprising and disturbing than the silence of most of the American Jewish leadership even after it became privy to Hitler's implementation of the Final Solution.

The issue remains moot whether or not local Jewish leaders in the towns and cities in Eastern Europe more or less "voluntarily" cooperated with the exterminators in determining who was sent to the camps, earlier or later. But we know, surely with the advantage of hindsight, that the American Jewish leadership in pursuing a policy of not "rocking the boat" enabled President Roosevelt and his State Department to pursue their priority of winning the war against Hitler without deflecting any resources, material or moral, to slow the Nazi extermination machine.

In the third year after V–E (Victory-in-Europe) day, the United Nations (UN) voted to establish the state of Israel, which set the stage, after an interregnum of two millennia, for Jewish hegemony in a major part of the Holy Land. This great victory following close on the heels of the

Holocaust goes far to explain how American Jewry and the Jews of other nations that were not in the path of the Nazi war machine were not totally demoralized by the mass murder of 6 million of their fellow Jews. The fact that the slaughter became generally known only at war's end gave it an unreality second only to the magnitude of the evil that had taken place.

This greatly encapsulated account of the momentous events of the last half century affecting Jews and Jewish communities must also take note of the fate of the Jews in the Soviet Union (USSR). Drawing on centuries-old Russian tradition of virulent anti-Semitism, the Communist leadership has found it expedient to discriminate against Jews as individuals and to restrict severely their opportunities for career advancement; to outlaw all Jewish efforts at communal activity — religious, cultural, and other; and to sponsor the preparation, publication, and dissemination of virulent anti-Jewish and anti-Israel propaganda for both internal and international (mostly Muslim) markets. But that is not the whole of the story. The USSR voted in the UN in 1948 in favor of establishing the state of Israel: in the early 1970s and again in the late 1970s it facilitated the outmigration of tens of thousands of Russian Jews to Israel and to the West. And in mid-1988 there are signs that its anti-Israel, anti-Jewish policies may again be moderated.

I have called attention to three momentous events: the Holocaust; the establishment of the state of Israel; the holding hostage of Soviet Jews. The question that remains is how I plan to deal with these world-shattering events. I spent a year and a half in Germany as a student at Heidelberg University (1928–29), only a few years before the street-brawling Nazis succeeded in toppling the Weimar Republic, thereby setting the stage for the Final Solution. In chapter 4 I draw on my firsthand experiences and observations about the early days of the Nazi bid for power in the hope that these experiences can add a little insight to the immensity of the evil that continues to challenge our understanding.

My exposures to the problems of the Yishuv (the Jews engaged in building their homeland in Palestine) and later to the young and maturing state of Israel have been many and continuing, and again I hope that the facts and the interpretations that I venture in chapter 8 may add some new perspectives.

There is no chapter on the Jews in Soviet Russia, since I have had no opportunity to become informed about their plight other than through secondary sources and through occasional discussions with refugees.

This book is first and foremost a personal view of selected aspects of major events in the lives of American Jews informed by my background, my discipline, my lengthened perspective and, finally, my own set of values, which helped me to cope sometimes more and sometimes less successfully with both my Jewish and my American roots.

I will start with my background, which is the focus of the next chapter. Even though I opted in my youth for playing baseball over studying Hebrew, and for the most part succeeded in winning that struggle with my parents, and even though until my adolescence I was critical about my father's pattern of work and life — he didn't know who Babe Ruth was and he never went (at that time) to the movies — I learned by osmosis a great deal about all things Jewish, past and present; a process of learning that accelerated on my return from Heidelberg, which still left me twenty-four years in which to deepen my intellectual relationship with my father before he died.

I have written at length about my father in *Keeper of the Law: Louis Ginzberg* (1966). While he would probably question and often disagree about many points of fact and interpretation, this present book has his initials on every page. In a moment of rare intimacy — because he was a very private person — my father remarked that, had his father been alive, he would not have been able to publish his three-volume life's work — *A Commentary on the Palestinian Talmud* (1941) — because my grandfather would have considered his critiques of the great rabbinic masters and his reconstructions of the sacred texts unacceptable.

We know in this post-Freudian age that sons do not settle accounts with their fathers nearly so easily and neatly as the preceding paragraphs suggest. My father's existence was based on three mutually reinforcing commitments: the survival of the Jewish people was his overriding goal; a respect for Jewish law and tradition was the foundation of his life; and a dedication to Jewish scholarship was his lodestar.

I surely absorbed from my father a respect for the historicity of the Jewish people, but in my case the understanding was more intellectual than emotional. I recall my father's crying out loud when he read the prayers on Tishabov at the little synagogue in Waterville, Maine, with a sense of immediacy that he himself had been present at each of the tragic events that the fast-day recalled. He was part of a living continuity with the Jews of earlier ages. In my case, it was more a matter of understanding than of feeling.

How does my training as an economist and my research specialty of human resources help me to deal insightfully with the themes that comprise this book? One of the central phenomena that provides the spine for this analysis is the impressive gains in education, occupational status, and income that American Jews have been able to achieve in the post-World War II era. Clearly an economist, with a special interest in human resources, is better positioned than most to unravel what happened and

why; at a minimum such a person should be innoculated against accepting facile interpretations. But the links between my specialty and my
interest in Jewish affairs have been much closer and more direct. Let me
illustrate.

My first formal connection with any Jewish organization was in helping to establish in the mid-1930s the Jewish Occupational Council of
which Morris Raphael Cohen, the distinguished philosopher at City College of New York, was the founding head. Until the advent of Adolf
Hitler, Cohen had distanced himself from Jewish activities and had
adopted in his classroom a mocking if not hostile attitude toward those of
his students who were affirming Jews. But he early realized that Hitler's
doctrines could leap over borders and oceans and threaten the United
States. Faced as the country was by intractably high levels of unemployment, it was important for Jews as individuals and as members of an
exposed minority to consider carefully their options with respect to their
education and career choices. Cohen, with his East European roots,
concluded that too many American Jews were crowding into a limited
number of service fields, making them potentially vulnerable. I do not
recall a great deal about the nature and scope of the council's work, but I
remember that I recruited the first director, Professor Albert Abraham-
son of the Economics Department of Bowdoin College, who got the
council off to a good start.

About a quarter of a century later I was in Jerusalem on one of my
many missions on behalf of the United States or the Israeli government.
My visit coincided with the monthly meeting of the Study Group on
Contemporary Jewish Issues, which Professor Moshe Davis of the Hebrew University had organized and which met at the home of the president of Israel, at the time Yitzhack Ben-Zvi. I was asked to speak and
selected as my theme "The Changing Occupational Status of American
Jews."

I have no detailed recollection of what I said, but I vividly recall the
stormy discussion that followed. Most of those present, and particularly
the oldsters such as Ben-Zvi, refused to accept my basic propositions:
that American Jews had secured a strong niche for themselves in the
American economy, which, if the economy did not falter, assured them a
favorable economic future; that it was fortunate that the Jews were vastly
"overrepresented" in professional and service occupations, for that was
the direction in which the U.S. economy was headed; that the relatively
small number of American Jews in basic industries, particularly agriculture, manufacturing, and construction, was a sign not of weakness but of
strength. While Ben-Zvi was too polite an individual and host to tell me
outright that I was naïve, even foolish, he hinted at what he considered to

be the preeminent lesson of Jewish history—the inevitable decline and collapse, sooner or later, of every Jewish community in the Diaspora no matter how great its prior accomplishments. Why should the United States be different from Alexandria, Spain, Lithuania, Germany?

There have always been major differences among Jews as to how they interpret their past, how they evaluate their present circumstances, and what they anticipate in the future. But never were such differences greater than among Eastern European Jewry during the half century between 1880 and the coming to power of Hitler in 1933. Over 2 million came to America and some tens of thousands went to Palestine. Several million were trapped inside Russia once the Communists took over. That left several million more, mostly in Poland and in southeastern Europe, covering the spectrum from the ultra-Orthodox to alienated modernists.

Ben-Zvi, more Hebraist than politician, was certain that sooner or later the Diaspora would once again play the Jews false and their only security was, while they still had time, to relocate in Israel. The fact that this "theory" was outside the experience and expectations of American Jews made no difference. Committed Zionists, like other committed people, have a corner on the truth. I learned early not to argue with those who know that theirs is the only right answer.

From one perspective, all of my assignments for Jewish organizations in the United States, in Israel, and most recently for World ORT (Organization for Rehabilitation through Training) have been directly related to my field of specialization. I early decided to respond affirmatively to any reasonable request from any Jewish organization whose program I respected even if it did not square with all or even most of my preconceptions and preferences.

In 1941 I served as the second director of the Allotment Committee for the United Jewish Appeal (UJA). After many years of negotiation, the American Jewish Joint Distribution Committee, which had concentrated its philanthropic efforts on assisting Jews and Jewish communities in the Diaspora, and the United Palestine Appeal, which devoted itself to building up the homeland, joined forces for fund-raising purposes in the hope and expectation that a combined effort would result in a larger total sum and reduced costs of operations. The two agreed on a formula to divide a predetermined minimum and left open till later the distribution of the remainder. That decision was to be made by an Allotment Committee of seven members, composed of two representatives from each of the principals and three neutrals. As director of research, my analysis was to guide the Allotment Committee. I had one assistant, Isaiah Frank, who went on to have a distinguished career, first in the Department of State and later as the William L. Clayton Professor of International Economic

Studies at the Johns Hopkins School of Advanced International Studies in Washington, D.C.

Of the seven members on the Allotment Committee, I reacted most strongly to Rabbi Abba Hillel Silver, whose behavior, bargaining tactics, and language were totally at variance with what I knew and expected from a leading member of the rabbinate. I quickly recognized that he was a man of strong commitment and substantial talent, but I never was able to accept his bullying tactics, disingenuousness, and ruthlessness. But then I was young and this was my first experience with organizational infighting.

A more constructive recollection that I retain from that assignment was my persuading Milton Friedman to develop a preliminary estimate of the distribution of income among American Jews. On the basis of his estimates I concluded that only a small proportion of potential donors was contributing to the joint appeal, and that the prospects for raising additional sums was much greater than even an aggressive bureaucrat such as Henry Montor had realized. But Montor shortly thereafter raised his sights and his goals and kept raising them, and in the process proved that the potential for additional giving was indeed substantial (see my *Report to American Jews: On Overseas Relief, Palestine and Refugees in the U.S.*, 1942).

Shortly after my return from war service, Dr. I. S. Wechsler, the distinguished neurologist and a long-term friend of my family, asked me to join the Executive Committee of the American Friends of the Hebrew University, the chair of which he had recently assumed. Over the next years I tried to be helpful, but was able to contribute relatively little, since it took Wechsler many years to attract wealthy and devoted laypersons to the board. But at one point I was able to assure that the negotiations between the Hebrew University and a young economist from the Midwest, Don Patinkin, did not fall through as had so many prior negotiations between principals 6,000 miles distant from each other. Patinkin moved to Jerusalem and over the years developed an outstanding department of economics at the Hebrew University and trained two generations of able economists. It was surely not his fault that the Israeli government has until recently made infrequent use of this talent pool. Patinkin has served both as rector and as president of the university, retiring in 1986 from the last post when the exploding deficit of the university, dating largely from his predecessors, led to a forced change of the guard.

Shortly after I joined the Army Services Forces in September 1942, I met, through my former teacher at Columbia College, T. C. Blaisdell, Israel Sieff (later Lord Sieff) of Britain's Marks and Spencer, who was to become a close friend. While living in Washington, Sieff engaged in a number of activities, including efforts to enlarge British exports in order to increase Britain's capacity to wage war. But, as I soon learned, he was also deeply involved in advancing the development of Palestine.

Sieff took the lead in organizing a discussion group of economists, lawyers, and other government officials to look at the potential of Palestine at the war's end to absorb large numbers of refugee Jews who would need to be relocated. In late 1943 Sieff was called before a congressional committee to explain how an agent of the British government was also providing advice to Leon Henderson, the senior U.S. official in charge of the Office of Price Administration. The quality of the interrogation is suggested by the chairman's initiating the inquiry by asking the witness whether his full name was in truth *Israel Moses Sieff!* Shortly thereafter, Sieff returned to London and I assumed the chairmanship of the group.

Through the fund-raising efforts of Sieff's associate in the United States, M. H. Blinken, we were able to commission and publish a major study: *Palestine: Problem and Promise* (1946) by Robert Nathan, Oscar Gass, and Daniel Creamer, which put to rest the many questions about the "absorptive capacity of Palestine." It is worth noting that Blinken, in his money-raising activities, was able to obtain a contribution of $10,000 from Lessing Rosenwald of Sears, who up to that point had been in the vanguard of the anti-Zionists. Blinken explained that ours was a serious scholarly inquiry, not an exercise in propaganda.

The only diplomatic mission that I carried out for the United States was to serve in the spring of 1946 as the U.S. representative to the Five-Power Conference on Non-Repatriable Refugees. In the major reparations conference of late 1945 the U.S. delegation, largely under the promptings of my close friend Moses Abramovitz, succeeded in adding a special provision aimed at facilitating the relocation of nonrepatriable refugees. Three sources of funds were identified: $25 million to be contributed by Germany; nonmonetary gold (the jewelry and teeth fillings of concentration-camp victims); heirless funds on deposit in Swiss and other foreign banks. The recovery and distribution of these funds were left to a successor Five-Power Conference to be composed of representatives of the United States, the United Kingdom, France, Czechoslovakia, and Yugoslavia.

This is not the place to tell the story in full of how the State Department at the last moment tried to persuade me not to go to Europe in the face of Mrs. Eleanor Roosevelt's lack of success at a UN commission meeting in London to obtain agreement from the Eastern bloc (Yugoslavia) on the definition of a refugee; David Ben-Gurion's willingness to settle with me before the convening of the conference for one penny on $1,000; Ernest Bevin's not delivering on a promise by his secretary of state, Hector McNeil, to provide 2,000 permits to resettle orphans in Palestine; the anti-Jewish orientation of the International Relief Organization, which my friend Patrick Murphy Malin headed; and how I persuaded the Yugoslavians to support the U.S. position with the result that the Jewish Agency and the Joint Distribution Committee eventually received (after several years) about 90 percent of some $60 million of reparations to resettle nonrepatriable Jewish refugees primarily in Palestine, to the great surprise of all concerned — the State Department, our allies, Ben-Gurion and, not least, myself.

In 1948 Blinken asked me to write a background paper that could serve as a discussion piece to help the American Jewish leadership reassess where they were and where they should be heading with their complementary and competing organizations, a task made more urgent by the establishment of the State of Israel. By mid-1949 I had a draft of *Agenda for American Jews* completed, which Columbia University Press published in 1950. It was more an annotated outline than a book; within 100 small pages I analyzed the challenges facing the principal institutions of American Jews: synagogue, philanthropy, defense agencies, Israel.

The monograph was never used as intended. The lay leadership, preoccupied with raising money for good causes, saw no need to address, much less answer, the many difficult questions that I had raised. But the *Agenda* went through a number of printings, since it was picked up for adult study, mostly by Conservative and Reconstructionist groups. And it came to enjoy a special dividend. Professor Moshe Davis of the Hebrew University had it translated into Hebrew and used it for years as a basic text to help orient his successive classes to the problems confronting American Jews. And in 1980 Schocken Publishing House, Tel Aviv, published a volume of mine entitled *American Jews: The Building of a Voluntary Community* (in Hebrew) which consisted of the *Agenda* and a dozen or more recent articles of mine in and around the same theme. Although I made one or two efforts to bring the *Agenda* up to date, including my contribution to the *Festschrift* prepared for Professor Davis (1984), this book is in part the belated response to a challenge that I had long recognized but had not earlier been able to meet.

Most of my extracurricular activities in the 1950s with respect to Jewish issues were centered in and around Israel (see chapter 8) except for my membership on the Publication Committee of the Jewish Publication Society. The Publication Committee was an awkward instrument for recommending manuscripts for publication, since it contained too many members with diverse ideologies, tastes, and scholarly standards. I was asked to undertake a management study and my radical recommendation to transform the committee into an advisory body to the editor and board was to my great surprise accepted. My other activities were limited to occasional presentations to conventions of the Rabbinical Assembly on the role of the rabbi in a rapidly changing American scene; and some lectures and articles growing out of my *Agenda* book that focused on the organizational problems of Jewish life.

In 1960 I undertook the first of two special inquiries for the Federation of Jewish Philanthropies (FJP) in New York City—a reassessment of the FJPs hospitals and health-care institutions in the face of changes in demography, residential patterns, and the economics of health care. The chair of the committee to which I reported was Judge Henry Friendly, a man of high intelligence, great commitment, and real warmth. The friendship between the Friendlys and the Ginzbergs that followed this assignment provided an extra dividend.

It is difficult for me, even in retrospect, to assess the value of the 1961 study that Peter Rogatz and I produced, *Planning for Better Hospital Care.* Lawrence Wien, the then president of the Federation of Jewish Philanthropies, recalled on several occasions his astonishment at, and disbelief of, our forecast that hospital expenditures would increase by 35 percent within the next three to five years. The actual increase proved our estimate to be low. In the short run, our major recommendations — to tie Einstein School of Medicine more closely to Montefiore Hospital, to encourage closer relations between Maimonides and Brooklyn Jewish Hospital, and to transfer the Hospital for Joint Diseases to the city — were not acted on, at least not then. Our greatest impact came from a throw-away sentence to the effect that a major teaching hospital that wanted to remain at the cutting edge had to have a close affiliation with a medical school. The Mt. Sinai Hospital physicians used that sentence to persuade its trustees that, since they did not have such a close relationship, the trustees should establish a medical school. Gustav Levy, the key trustee, was informed that the cost would approximate $10 million. When in the mid-1970s he quoted this original figure, the total had already exceeded $140 million!

An aside: there was surely nothing in our report to suggest that, if and when Mt. Sinai Hospital and the potential medical school were to be integrated into a Mt. Sinai Medical Center under a president, all of the successive incumbents would be non-Jews, but that is what happened.

I came away from this FJP assignment with conflicting views of the state of Jewish philanthropy. I was impressed with the seriousness with which many trustees carried out their responsibilities. I found the two senior bureaucrats, Maurice Hexter and Joseph Willen, men of considerable skill with records of outstanding performance. But the federation, as its name denotes, was just that — a loose association of a large number of voluntary health and social welfare organizations whose leaders had to maneuver carefully in order not to alienate any important constituency. When Friendly and I met with the trustees of the Hospital for Joint Diseases and pointed out to them the desirability of their taking early action to divest themselves of their building at 124th Street in the middle of Harlem, they heard us out but their critique of our proposal quickly indicated that they had no intention of considering it carefully and even less of going along with our recommendation. Many years and much trouble had to intervene before the trustees facing a no-win situation had to flee the neighborhood and relocate their core orthopedic activities at Beth Israel Hospital in lower Manhattan.

About a decade later I found myself once again carrying out an assignment for the FJP. This time my charge was to assess how the federation should restructure and strengthen its community-wide financial support for Jewish education. Specifically, the federation trustees wanted me to look closely at the Board of Jewish Education, the instrumentality through which it had long funneled its modest support for education.

The explosive growth of Jewish day schools and the recent broadening and deepening of interest in Jewish subjects in the many colleges and universities in the New York area as well as elsewhere (see chapter 9) presented a major financial challenge to the federation, which was hard-pressed to meet the expanding budgetary requests from its hospital and social welfare agencies.

Although I was not impressed with the track record of the Board of Jewish Education, I took pains to recommend reforms rather than a radical restructuring, since I realized that the leaders who were pressing for more assistance to Jewish education were tied to the board, while mainline FJP trustees, with few exceptions, were cautious or hostile to expanding their responsibilities for Jewish education.

I am not sure that I provided the FJP trustees with the blueprint they needed to restructure their financing of Jewish education. But one thing is clear. The timing was wrong. The report was reviewed, read by a few interested parties, and buried. But with the passage of time and under the continuing prodding from the more aggressive Orthodox constituencies and lubricated by Joseph Gruss's substantial earmarked contributions, the FJP has assumed a more prominent role in the financing of Jewish education.

In the early 1970s Louis Finkelstein, a favorite and talented student of my father's and later his colleague, was ready to step down from the chancellorship of the Jewish Theological Seminary, which he had held for thirty years. I had earlier served as a sounding board for Gerson Cohen when the seminary sought (and succeeded) in luring him back from

Columbia University where he had spent some years as the successor to Salo Baron. In the selection process precipitated by Finkelstein's retirement, I served once again as a sounding board for Cohen, but this time I also sought to persuade the decision-makers that they had to give the nod to Cohen, whose qualifications far outdistanced the others in the running. In June 1986 Cohen resigned the chancellorship. In chapter 10 I comment on the changing position of the Seminary—the flagship of the Conservative movement—over the eighty-six years since its reorganization in 1902.

In 1982 I was invited to give the Jules Backman Lecture at the Hebrew Union College, my first visit to the lead institution of the Reform movement. I was startled to find faculty members who wore yarmulkas, a sizable group of devout students participating in morning services, including women students who were enrolled in the program leading to ordination as rabbis, and many more signs that revealed how far the Reform movement had come from its turn-of-the-century orientation with its bravado of eating forbidden food, holding services in English on Sunday, and propagating the view that the essence of Judaism was to be found in religion and ethics, not in law, custom, tradition, shared history, and a love of Zion. It was a powerful reminder that no segment of Jewish experience, such as the Reform movement in the United States at its zenith (1880–1920), is impervious to radical change within a relatively short period of time, a very short period when placed alongside the more than three millennia of recorded Jewish history.

In 1984 Professor William Haber, a long-term friend from the University of Michigan, asked me to join a newly organized Academic Advisory Committee to World ORT for the purpose of providing guidance to its far-flung occupational schools in France, North Africa, Latin America, and especially Israel, a system that has contributed so much over more than a century to assisting young Jews to acquire skills and competences that ease their entrance into good jobs and careers. In the company of distinguished colleagues from the United States, the United Kingdom, France, Latin America, and Israel, I have found this new assignment an excellent opportunity to learn more about the problems facing young Jews in different parts of the world as they prepare themselves for jobs and careers and to make some modest contributions to strengthening the educational programming to which they are exposed.

As noted earlier this book is an effort at personal evaluation of the changing roles and prospects of American Jews in a century characterized by many challenges and opportunities. Accordingly it may be illuminating to call attention to a number of events that I had not anticipated when I published my *Agenda* in 1950.

The exercise will be a reminder to both the writer and the reader to proceed with caution before reaching conclusions about any aspect of the American Jewish experience, since the time period is so miniscule a part of the recorded history of the Jews. Without ascribing any significance to their ordering, I shall list each of the unexpected developments and briefly explain what is surprising, at least to me, about each.

The presence, growth, and influence of the Hasidic immigrants and the concomitant growth of the American-born Orthodox were largely if not totally hidden from my view in 1950. The strong religious, educational, and cultural institutions of the Orthodox have begun not only to alter the shape of Jewish life in the cities where they are concentrated, such as New York, Cleveland, Chicago, and Los Angeles, but have also become, as we shall see, a significant factor in the ongoing development of the state of Israel.

I recall calling on Dr. Chaim Weizmann in 1947 in the company of my friend Eliahu Eilat, then resident representative of the Jewish Agency in Washington, a few hours after President Harry Truman had turned down Weizmann's request that the United States not support the trusteeship proposal then pending before the UN Security Council. I had known Dr. Weizmann for the better part of a decade and had seen him in many situations where the outcome of the cause he was pleading looked bleak. But that evening he was severely depressed and remarked that he would never again set foot in the United States. I knew through my ties with the Pentagon of General George C. Marshall's judgment that if it came to armed conflict between Jews and Arabs, the Yishuv would be destroyed. I discussed General Marshall's views with Weizmann, who explained to me that General Marshall was misreading the situation in the Middle East. The Arabs were in disarray and with luck it would take them the better part of a half century or more to sort themselves out, an essential precondition to establishing effective governments. That was the half century that the Jews needed to secure their state. With the benefit of hindsight, it is clear that Dr. Weizmann had a deeper understanding of the Middle East than General Marshall. But even Weizmann did not anticipate that in 1979 the president of the United States, Jimmy Carter, would travel thousands of miles to obtain Anwar Sadat's and Menachem Begin's agreement to the terms of a treaty of peace between Egypt and Israel. And Weizmann would have been even more surprised that in 1985 the United States signed an important agreement with Israel to coordinate military planning in the area.

In the *Agenda* I had taken a critical view of the activities of the principal Jewish "defense" organizations in the United States — the American Jewish Committee, the American Jewish Congress, and the Anti-Defamation League of the B'nai B'rith. It seemed to me to be a wasteful use of scarce resources to attempt to change the attitudes of Gentiles toward Jews, since in my view such an effort was doomed to failure.

But I had not allowed for the impact of what one liberal pope, John XXIII, in the aftermath of the Holocaust, could accomplish to bring about a fundamental change in Catholic doctrine and behavior with respect to the Jews. Vatican Council II finally lifted the charge of deicide from the Jews—the fuel that fed European anti-Semitism for two millennia. And John Paul II, cut from a more conservative mold, underscored in 1986 that the shift in Catholic doctrine would not be reversed when, for the first time in the history of the papacy, a pope visited a synagogue and participated in an ecumenical service.

The last surprise relates to the rapid lowering and disappearance of so many discriminatory barriers that American Jews had previously encountered in higher education, corporate life, social institutions, the professions, and politics. In the early post-World War II years, when we still did a little skiing, I suggested to my wife that she telephone an inn in Stowe, Vermont, to inquire whether they had accommodations and specifically whether they accepted Jews. To her surprise, but not to mine, she was turned down. But I was surprised a year later when, after my friend at Lockheed had arranged for us to spend some days in Apple Valley in the California desert, the room clerk couldn't find our reservation. And as late as 1954 when we first found a summer home on Martha's Vineyard, the real estate agent explained to us that we had better concentrate our search up-island, in the Chilmark area, since we "wouldn't be happy in Edgartown." When Abba Eban, Israel's first ambassador to the United Nations and the United States, wanted to get away for a complete rest, David Niles, an assistant to President Truman, found him accommodations at the Harborside Inn in Edgartown, which he assured Eban, would provide the isolation he was seeking.

In the early 1950s the staff of the American Jewish Committee (AJC) consulted me about possible actions it might take to increase the number of Jews admitted to medical school. I explained that demography had taken care of the issue. The small size of the college-age cohort assured that well-qualified Jews were being accepted at U.S. medical schools.

As an alternative I suggested that the AJC look into anti-Semitism in the executive suite and I steered it to DuPont, among other large companies. I was later informed that a senior DuPont official explained to the representatives of the AJC that the corporation did not discriminate. However, the company had a rule that its top officials had to be members of the Wilmington Country Club and the club regrettably followed an exclusionary policy. It was not all that many years later that Irving Shapiro became DuPont's chief executive officer!

When Michael Dukakis first announced his intention to pursue the Democratic party's nomination for the presidency, I considered the odds against his winning either or both the nomination and the election to be very high, of the order of one in ten. I did not believe that large sections of the American electorate, especially in the South and the Midwest, would respond positively to a candidate of Greek extraction who was married to a Jew. Clearly my concerns, heavily influenced by my recollections of the hostility directed at Alfred E. Smith in 1928 and John F. Kennedy in 1960 — solely on the grounds of their Catholicism — had oversensitized me to the virulence of religious and ethnic prejudice. Here is a potent reminder that a lengthened perspective can be more liability than asset. At least I have put myself on warning to recalculate the changing fulcrum between continuity and change.

There is no need to pile evidence upon evidence to prove that the four decades following the end of World War II witnessed the removal of most if not all barriers in the path of Jews who want to compete for the major prizes in American life. This does not mean, of course, that prejudice against Jews has disappeared, but it does mean that its institutionalized practice has been greatly diminished. Whether like Banquo's ghost it may reappear at a later date will be discussed in the final chapter.

2

My Father's Influence

My father died on November 9, 1953, shortly before his eightieth birthday as a result of a cerebral hemorrhage that had set in less than eighteen hours earlier. Just before he was stricken, he spoke to me about a report that the *New York Times* carried that morning. He said that he didn't like "Bible-touting secretaries of state." That was strong language for a man to whom the Bible meant so much. But then, the Jews and Judaism meant even more to him. John Foster Dulles must have been up to one of his many tricks in the Middle East, which my father believed didn't augur well for Israel.

My father's knowledge of and feeling for the Bible is revealed by the following two anecdotes. He told friends that as a youngster of six or seven he had won bets that stipulated that, given any phrase in the Bible, he could recite the passage that followed. The more revealing tale was told to me by Professor Moshe Davis in Jerusalem some years after my father's death. Davis had been his student at the Seminary in the 1940s. During one of his lectures, my father started to quote a phrase from Job, stumbled, became agitated, stopped, and told his class that he would never lecture again. Fortunately, several students caught up with him as he was walking home and persuaded him that forgetting a phrase in the Bible was no justification for his prematurely ending his teaching career. They convinced him and he went on teaching until the time of his death.

I have brought my father into this account early and will report at some length about his views concerning the central issues of Jewish experience, because they are important in their own right and especially because they became the building blocks for my own approach. This chapter, then, will deal sequentially with three closely related elements: my father's views and conclusions about Jews and Judaism based on his long scholarly endeavors, including his appraisal of the momentous events that occurred in his later years. I shall then discuss the striking differences in the environments in which each of us grew up, in an effort to explain what part of his intellectual and emotional legacy I was able to absorb and put to good use and the part that I could not incorporate. Third, I shall briefly consider some of the major events that have occurred during the third of a century since my father's death that must be taken into account in assessing the future development of the Jews in the United States, Europe, and Israel.

My father immigrated to the United States in 1899 to accept a position at the Hebrew Union College, but the offer evaporated while he was on shipboard. The sentence leaves out as much as it has included. What needs to be added is that my father, despite his extraordinary talent and promise — his doctorate from Heidelberg carried the citation *superato* — had little or no prospect of finding a suitable job in Germany and he had earlier turned his back on Eastern Europe.

In 1902, after a stint as a senior editor of the *Jewish Encyclopedia*, he became the first faculty member whom Solomon Schechter appointed to the newly reorganized Jewish Theological Seminary. The anomalies in Jewish life and institutions that he experienced on his arrival in the United States were many — a Reform movement racing to throw off the last remnants of its Jewishness; the large numbers of Jewish immigrants from Eastern Europe willingly or reluctantly discarding the law and tradition as they set about to make a new life for themselves and their children; a small number of wealthy and concerned German Jews in leadership roles who sought to speed the acculturation of the new arrivals; the many smaller and larger blocs of Yiddishists, Bundists, Zionists, Orthodox, antireligious, and Ethical Culturists, each seeking a niche for themselves and their ideology.

A hard lesson, but one that my father learned quickly, was that in this frontier land the scholar did not have a leadership role. Power in the United States was in the hands of the banker, the merchant, the lawyer, occasionally the orator or the bureaucrat. Scholars were sidelined. But if each group was to go its own way, even to the point of ignoring or undermining the foundations — religion, law, tradition — that had held the Jews together for more than 2,000 years, the outlook for survival and vitality of the American Jewish community was bleak.

Over the half century that my father was a participant-observer in Jewish affairs, the pendulum swung away from anarchy toward stabilization. The Seminary fulfilled that part of its founding mission that was aimed at speeding the acculturation of the immigrants who wanted to continue practicing their religion while making suitable accommodations to the changes of time and place. Conversion never became a serious alternative. By the early 1940s most American Jews had become passive if not active Zionists. By then the Reform movement was taking several steps back toward tradition. Not to be minimized were the substantial gains that the Jewish population had achieved in improving its educational, occupational, economic, and social positions. As a result of these improvements, the Jewish community had been able to strengthen its own institutions and to assist Jewish communities abroad.

Notwithstanding all of these signs of normalization and improvement, my father retained many doubts about the future prospects of Judaism in the United States even in the last years of his life. He was unable to identify the sources for self-renewal and, more particularly, the sources of a future leadership committed to and knowledgeable about the written and the oral law who would have the opportunity and the desire to devote themselves to a life of scholarship. Without such a leadership that the community would support, cherish, and respect, he saw little hope for a vital Judaism in the United States. He knew that during his five decades at the Seminary he had been unable to train even a dozen dedicated scholars. He had many talented students but they went on to become active members of the rabbinate, a necessary but not in his view a sufficient condition to assure that Judaism would be able to remain vital in the decades ahead. Until the end of World War II, Judaism in the United States had been living off its European inheritance. Once East European Jewry had been exterminated he became even more concerned about the capacity of American Jewry to renew itself.

How did my father see the Orthodox — were they not a potential source of strength and renewal? My answer is a loud No. During prohibition he had been violently attacked by some of the Orthodox because he had written an opinion for the U.S. Treasury stating that nonfermented wine was suitable for ritual use, thereby jeopardizing the profitable illegal trade in sacramental wine. And he was no innocent concerning the ties among the kosher butchers, the supervisory rabbinate, and the gangsters in-between.

In the late 1920s a trial balloon went up among a few of the trustees whether or not the Seminary and the Yeshiva should be merged, ostensibly to broaden and deepen their combined resources. The cynics believed that the trustees were looking for a way to reduce their philanthropic burden. My father's opinion was elicited and he advised against further explorations. In his view there was no basis for an agreement between the two boards, the two faculties, the two constituencies.

Shortly after the end of World War II the leaders of his old alma mater, Telsch Yeshiva in Lithuania, were exploring opening a branch in Cleveland, Ohio, and they sought my father's help. He turned them down on the ground that such an effort was doomed to failure. In his view Telsch could not take root in American soil and it should therefore not make the attempt. Although emissaries came to plead with him he would not lend his name or encourage the effort.

He knew that for many years some of the best Seminary students were graduates of the Yeshiva in New York City or of one of the smaller Orthodox centers of Talmudic study around the country. But this was one-way traffic — from the small Orthodox right into the larger Conservative center. My father did not see much of a future for Orthodoxy in this country. This belief, when added to his unease about the Conservative movement and his distaste for Reform, helps to explain why he was pessimistic about the future of Judaism in the United States.

My father had been born in Kovno, Lithuania, in 1873 and spent the first seven years of his life there. His father, a merchant-scholar, then relocated the family for two years in Klin (near Moscow). Young Louis later continued his studies at Telsch and Vilna. Proud of his lineage studded with great scholars, including the Gaon of Vilna whose name I bear, he was able to trace the Ginzberg family back to Günzburg (between Augsburg and Ulm) where they had settled early in the sixteenth century after migrating over the Alps from Padua. In 1929 I spent a day walking around Günzburg, which struck me as a town with no special charm but also with no special liabilities. But that was before the world became acquainted with the evil Dr. Josef Mengele, who was a native of Günzburg.

My father's basic endowment was the distilled essence of Lithuanian Jewish learning and experience. As I reflect on his early years, two points impress me as being of more than casual interest. In his large repertoire of stories, he seldom mentioned native Lithuanians. He clearly had had little or no contact with them. And the same is true of his reportage of the two years that he lived in the vicinity of Moscow: once again, there was no reference to the local population. Moreover, although he was a gifted linguist who wrote in eight languages, he had forgotten what little Russian he had picked up and he knew not a word of Lithuanian.

My other reflection is more tantalizing, for it relates directly to an understanding of himself, his values, and his goals. Within a year after his father had moved the family to Amsterdam in the mid-1880s, my father, who had been left behind to pursue his Talmudic studies, managed to escape by arranging to visit his parents. He never returned to Lithuania except once to spend a few days with his favorite grandmother on the occasion of her ninetieth birthday. At fifteen he began his secular education in Frankfurt am Main and, after studying at the universities of Berlin and Strassburg, he took his doctorate at Heidelberg. He left Europe in 1899 to relocate in the United States.

He came to know the Germans well and during his university days he wrote for the *Frankfurter Zeitung* to help support himself. As soon as Hitler became chancellor in early 1933, my father saw only trouble and more trouble ahead for the Jews. He had an expert's knowledge of the depth of German anti-Semitism and he recognized that once the political leadership decided to give it free rein, only catastrophe could follow. But my father had studied with Theodore Nöldeke in Strassburg for four years and considered him to be the greatest Semitic scholar of all times and a man without an ounce of prejudice. He had listened to lectures by Rudolph Virchow in Berlin and he was acquainted with a number of other Germans of talent and genius to whom Jew-baiting was an anathema.

Even after my father had become aware of the magnitude of the Holocaust, he opposed the Morgenthau Plan to turn postwar Germany into an agricultural nation. He knew firsthand that not all Germans were Nazis and he saw no point in making it easier for Communist Russia to dominate Europe. At the time of the Harvard Tercentenary (1936), when he was one of the recipients of an honorary degree, he granted two interviews to a Hearst reporter. In the first, he accused the British of aggravating the Arab-Jewish conflict in Palestine to make their own position more secure. In his second interview, he warned about misreading the Russian Revolution and emphasized the ruthlessness of the Soviet leaders. Long knowledgeable about Karl Marx's virulent anti-Semitism, the more painful because Marx and he shared a rabbinical ancestor, he had been kept well informed about the rapidly worsening conditions of Soviet Jewry through the frequent visits to the USSR of his friend Professor Solomon Zeitlin. The Common Front of 1936 notwithstanding, my father contended that Hitler was using Stalin for his model in shaping his program of genocide, an approach that my father saw rooted in Russian history. I remember my chagrin at finding my father aligning himself with the most extreme critics of the Communist experiment.

I had kept my distance from left-wing organizers and organizations largely because I was not a joiner and there was not all that much political activity on the Columbia University campus. But I surely shared the belief of the radicals that the U.S. economy was in dire trouble and I was far from convinced that Roosevelt had the answers. I remember my embarrassment at my father's attack on the USSR just at the start of the united front.

On further reflection, I realize that my distancing myself from the Communists and their allies stemmed from my close friendship with

Frank I. Schechter to whom this book is dedicated. Frank, the son of my father's sponsor and colleague, Solomon Schechter, was a distinguished lawyer in New York City specializing in trademark law. In 1929 his sister Amy was one of a group charged with the murder through shooting of the police chief in Gastonia, North Carolina. Frank devoted months of unremitting efforts before he succeeded in nolle-prossing the charge against his sister. His primary difficulty was not with the local criminal justice appartus but, rather, with the Communist lawyers who in his view with reckless disregard of their clients' interests sought to make political capital out of the event. This was a searing experience for Frank and unquestionably contributed to a deterioration in his physical condition, which led to his premature death. But I learned an important lesson early that stood me in good stead.

My father's relations to Zionism and the rebuilding of the homeland are another story. He attended the Sixth Zionist Congress in 1905 and voted against accepting Uganda as a substitute area for settlement. This was the counterproposal that had been put forward by some of the delegates when the prospects of negotiating with the Turkish government for large-scale immigration of Jews into Palestine was stalled. Why not have the Jews settle on virgin lands in Uganda? The lovers of Zion had a simple answer: Uganda was not Zion! Shortly thereafter, my father withdrew from active participation because, among other reasons, he had no stomach for organizational infighting.

I grew up in a household in which we teasingly referred to Louis Ginzberg as the "father of Hadassah." Henrietta Szold had started the movement shortly after my father announced his engagement to a German *fraulein* upon his return from Germany in the summer of 1908. There was little discussion about Zionism during most of the years that I was growing up and even less about the ceaseless maneuverings involving Weizmann-Brandeis-Lipsky-Szold and the others who sought to lead what was a movement in the United States more in name than in fact. It was not until Solomon Goldman, a favorite student of my father's, assumed the presidency of the Zionist Organization of America in the late 1930s and came to share confidences and seek comfort in his difficult assignment that Zionism became a subject for intense discussion. But my father had much earlier become directly involved with the Yishuv, particularly with the Hebrew University in Jerusalem.

My father spent his one and only sabbatical in 1928–29 as the first visiting professor of Halachah at the Hebrew University. After some years, this visit led to the Seminary's recruiting first H. L. Ginsberg as professor of Bible and later Saul Lieberman as professor of Talmud.

Near the end of my father's stay, Nahum Bialik made a special trip to Jerusalem to plead with my father that he remain in Palestine because, among other reasons, Bialik believed that the revival of Hebrew would be strengthened by my father's mastery of Talmudic prose. At fifty-six my father was too settled in his ways, and probably too unsettled by the competing ideologies that he saw no way of reconciling or even moderating, to accept Bialik's challenge. He once remarked that as long as he had his library (some 3,000 books) he could live anywhere, even in Tokyo. But Bialik got part of his wish: my father thereafter wrote primarily in Hebrew. In fact it was difficult for me to persuade my father to write an English introduction to his *Commentary on the Palestinian Talmud*, which he acknowledged only in his Hebrew preface, because, I suspect, he wanted me tied to him in the language that he considered basic to the survival of the Jews.

During my father's year at the Hebrew University I was at Heidelberg and received a number of letters from him telling me of his deep concern that the Zionist leaders were not reading the Arab press and were not paying adequate attention to the Arabs, a neglect that he felt would come back to haunt them, as in fact it has.

In 1933, together with two distinguished British Jewish academicians, Sir Philip Hartog and Dr. Radcliff Salomon of Cambridge University, my father returned to Palestine to seek a solution to a growing conflict between Judah Magnes, the president of the Hebrew University, and many of his faculty. This conflict had earlier spilled over and had involved Albert Einstein and Chaim Weizmann among others. The Commission of Inquiry did what it was established to do. It was able to moderate even if it could not completely resolve the conflict, and as a result of the commission's work the university was better positioned to continue its expansion. Although he was largely immune to the seduction of praise and honors, I am sure that the establishment of the Louis Ginzberg Chair in Talmud at the Hebrew University in honor of his eightieth birthday, which he missed by three weeks, is the one recognition that would have pleased him greatly.

I must take note of a number of other strongly held views of my father, which left an indelible impression on me and which helped to shape my own point of departure in this assessment of the experiences of twentieth-century Jews in the United States and abroad.

My father believed that the Lithuanian Jewry of his youth was in spirit and in life the direct descendant of Pharisaic Judaism before the destruction of the Second Temple. My recollection is that he believed that a higher proportion of Lithuanian Jews, surely in the earlier part of the nineteenth century before the Enlightenment had begun to make inroads, lived a life more congruent with the law and tradition than did many Palestinian Jews around the time of the Common Era.

Impressed with the continuity of the law as the glue not only for survival but for regeneration, he moved with great circumspection in taking any action to weaken it. The following speak to this.

One of his favorite pupils, for whom he had high regard, was Rabbi Louis M. Epstein of Boston, who spent many years studying the Agunah question — the deserted wife who was unable to remarry because there was no definite proof that her husband was deceased. The Ginzberg family vacationed with the Epsteins for many summers in Maine, and Epstein talked extensively about the problem, but my father always shied away from approving any of the alternative solutions that Epstein proffered.

With the advantage of a lengthened perspective, I am sure that the solution that Professor Lieberman eventually worked out for the Rabbinical Assembly of a prenuptial delegation of authority to a Jewish court to dissolve a marriage without the presence and consent of the husband — or some similar arrangement — had been considered by my father but rejected on the ground that it would not be acceptable to the Orthodox rabbis abroad. He was determined not to contribute to schisms.

Confirmation of this interpretation can be found in my mother's periodically reminding my father that he should have gone ahead with his tentative plan to explore the calling of a Sanhedrin in Paris at the end of World War I to address the Agunah and similar Halachic questions that required reassessment in light of the turmoil wrought by the war and its aftermath. I am sure that my father's idea remained stillborn because he saw no prospect of finding a middle ground between the Orthodox and himself.

In the months preceding the establishment of the state of Israel, Eliahu Eilat had several extended conversations with my father about how the new government might deal with the problem of Jewish law in a secular state. In contrast to his hesitations about changing the law in the Diaspora, he was much more venturesome about modifications and adaptations in a Jewish state. He stressed two points: the government *qua* government should respect tradition such as observing *kashruth* in the military, closing its offices on the Sabbath, and acting in accordance with tradition in its other public actions. He was sure that the rabbis would insist on retaining jurisdiction over family law — marriage, divorce, and death. He hoped that an accommodation could be worked out but he was prophetic in his premonitions that if the rabbis got into politics it would be bad for everybody — the state, religion, and the public.

Although my father taught prospective rabbis over a period of a half century and although he understood that most of them would in time make a contribution to shoring up tradition in an unfriendly environment, he remained equivocal about the American rabbinate. His unease was diffuse. He believed that some of the leading rabbinical orators were publicity-mad. He felt antagonistic toward those who kept searching for a new rationale for Judaism, such as his long-term colleague Mordecai M. Kaplan. My father resigned from the Committee on Jewish Law of the Rabbinical Assembly after he concluded that most of the members of the committee were unqualified to participate in such deliberations.

My father used both sophistication and humor as powerful antidotes to rigidity and extremism, but on the question of intermarriage he had no give whatever. A first cousin who had married a Brahmin lived within a stone's throw of our family. I never met her and when my father insisted that all of our extended family break relations with her, his injunction was followed by many if not all of our clan.

When his long-term friend and colleague David Blondheim, professor of Romance Languages at Johns Hopkins, married Eleanor Lansing Dulles, my father was in the vanguard of those who insisted that Blondheim relinquish his posts in Jewish organizations such as the American Academy of Jewish Research and the Jewish Publication Society. I am sure that my father was upset by Blondheim's suicide early in 1934 but that did not alter his attitude toward intermarriage. The first and only sign of a change came in his last years. He was very fond of a Gentile colleague of mine who had married a Jewish woman. When they were in the city, he always invited them to dinner. Professor Lieberman told me of several conversations that he had had with my father on the subject of intermarriage. In Lieberman's view the difference in their attitudes stemmed from the fact that my father's base of reference was Lithuania of the 1870s, while Lieberman's was Russia at the time of the revolution and immediately subsequent.

I have reflected now and again whether or not, in the absence of this immobile position of my father on intermarriage, I might have married one or another non-Jew with whom I kept company during the long period of my bachelorhood. My parents were acquainted with some of my women friends and on one birthday my mother and friend joined in buying me a gift. I know that my mother did not share my father's implacable hostility to my marrying out of the faith. On the other hand, I knew that such action on my part would result in a break with my father, a price that I had no intention of paying.

On further reflection I suspect that my keeping company with non-Jewish women was a strategy to prevent my marrying early, an action that did not fit my career plans. And I recall that when one of my Gentile friends was being importuned to accept an offer of marriage and consulted her psychoanalyst, she was told that I would never marry a non-Jew. When asked for comment, I confirmed what her analyst had told her. She accepted her marriage offer and shortly thereafter I started keeping company with a Jewish woman, recognizing that there was such a thing as too much caution. I was approaching my thirty-fifth birthday!

There was no possible way for me to tap into the deep reservoir of my father's emotional commitments to and knowledge of Jewish experience. But I was able to take some of his attitudes and learning and turn them into building blocks to guide myself.

No assessment of any Jewish community should be undertaken without consideration of the long and largely tragic histories of the many Jewish communities of earlier centuries. A shared religion, law, tradition, and language are the foundations for vitality and survival. Without them, no Diaspora community can survive, much less flourish. For millennia, the hope of return to Palestine was a binding force and a powerful reinforcing agent. Now that the state has been reestablished, it behooves all Jews to do their utmost to assure its security, survival, and further development.

It is easy for modernizers and acculturationists to seek an accommodation between the Halachah and the differing environments to which Jewish communities must adjust. But if basic ties to the past are severed, then the links between different communities in the Diaspora as well as between them and Israel may be jeopardized. The successful adjustment of tradition to a changing reality through time and space is the key to survival.

The roots of anti-Semitism are deeply embedded among all the peoples of Christendom, educated and uneducated alike. But latent and overt beliefs need not lead to destructive mass behavior. Nevertheless it is the better part of wisdom for Jews everywhere and at all times to remain alert to the possibility of hostile ideas leading to hostile actions.

These are the core lessons that I absorbed, not through study and reflection but largely by osmosis from one who had spent his life seeking to penetrate the deeper lessons of Jewish experience from the latter part of the Second Commonwealth to the mid-twentieth century, a period of over two millennia.

Let me set forth briefly several major forces on the American scene that were peripheral to my father's thought-ways but which have been part of my intellectual scaffolding.

The United States differs from Europe in that we are, to use FDR's words, a nation of immigrants. Since the Civil War over 45 million persons have immigrated. In the three decades before World War I (1880–1910) over 2 million Jews, mostly from Eastern Europe, came to the

United States and created the basis for what developed into the largest Diaspora community in the history of the Jews. It would be wrong to see the older American-born population, despite its open-gate policy, free of anti-Semitic feelings and actions, just as it would be wrong to assume that the non-Jewish immigrants left behind in Europe their ingrained hostile attitudes toward Jews. Nonetheless the demographic profile of the United States is characterized by a fluidity and ethnic and religious diversity that has no counterpart in any European country, a uniqueness that must be considered in assessing the evolution of the American Jewish community.

Another unique aspect of the United States is the long-term presence of a large black population (currently more than four times the size of the Jewish population), which has been severely oppressed and is still subject to widespread discrimination. The long stark division in Europe between the dominant Christian majorities and the relatively small Jewish minorities, only recently enfranchised, does not have a direct parallel in the United States where lines of religious cleavage are confounded by racial and ethnic divisions.

A third distinctive characteristic of life in the United States is the proliferation of voluntary organizations of all types, a phenomenon that was first noted by European visitors early in the nineteenth century. One may have serious reservations about a Judaism founded on federations and other money-raising agencies, defense organizations, political action groups, and an array of eleemosynary institutions, but these organizations provide the core experiences for group identification and commitment for many though not for all Jews.

Finally most of the preexisting barriers to interactions between Jews and the rest of the society have been lowered or removed. Native-born American Jews interact increasingly with non-Jews on every front: in school, at work, in political and social activities.

There were only four photos in my father's study, two of which spoke of his ties to non-Jews — a small snapshot of his teacher Nöldeke and one of George Foote Moore of Harvard University, whose third volume of *Judaism* contains many notes bracketed by the notation L. G. The others were a photo of the tombstone on his father's grave in Amsterdam, the Netherlands, and a large picture of Solomon Schechter. I recall, however, only two close relationships between the Ginzberg family and non-Jews during the twenty-two years that I lived at home. The first was with Theodore Benzinger, the distinguished Palestinian archeologist, who lost his professorship at Toronto University because of his German citizenship in World War I. My parents befriended him and after the war's end he returned to Europe as professor at Riga.

The other grew out of a proximity of cottages on Lake Messalonskee in central Maine. Frederick Fassett, Jr., a professor of English at the Massachusetts Institute of Technology (MIT) and his family became close friends of the Ginzbergs, and for years I was a special beneficiary of that relationship because Fred generously edited several of my early books.

I grew up in an area that was known at the time as Washington Heights and which today is designated as West Harlem. I have thought back about the boys with whom I grew up, attended school, and played ball. While Jews were probably in the majority, two of our five stick-ball team were non-Jews. My closest friend from the start of junior high school was of Scottish extraction. Almost all of my teachers in Public School 186, Speyer Junior High School, and DeWitt Clinton were Gentiles. One of my duties in high school was to alert the Gentile students to approaching Jewish holidays so that they could cut classes along with their Jewish friends.

Except when I had to accompany my father on Saturdays and Jewish holidays to the seminary synagogue, which I did with regularity between my sixth and thirteenth years, I had little awareness of belonging to a minority group. Synagogue kept me from playing ball on Saturday and holiday mornings but the afternoons found me out on the street with the team.

Since ours was an observant home, we had to ask the elevator man to turn lights, on the Sabbath, on and off and when there was a new attendant I recall a modicum of self-consciousness in explaining the request. And I was definitely self-conscious on Yom Kippur when my father attired in a cutaway wore sneakers, since leather, an animal derivative, was prohibited.

The only incident during my ten years in the public school system that focused on a Jewish issue related to my high school honor society's (Arista's) discussion as to where to hold its annual dinner. The question was whether it should be kosher or not. The arguments were coming loud and fast on both sides until a black student by the name of Casminsky asked for the floor and explained that he favored "kasha" because that was the way his grandmother cooked and he liked it. I later elicited from Casminsky that his ancestors had been the slaves of a Jewish plantation owner in the Caribbean.

As I reflect on what really went on in my parents' home, more particularly my childhood and early adolescent experiences with religion, Judaism, and matters of Jewish moment, I realize that the foregoing selective incidents don't do justice to my developmental process, emotionally or intellectually. Some additional data should be presented.

First, with respect to my learning Hebrew: my mother was my first

teacher but she gave up after a few months, recognizing that I was recalci-
trant and she was not cut out to teach. My father took over and tried hard
for years, not months, but with only modest success. I recalled that I
deeply resented that my lessons cut into my ball-playing time and I turned
surly. My usual excuse was to develop cramps early in the lesson period,
repair to the bathroom and devote some thirty to forty minutes pitching
pennies. With the canniness of the young I had discovered my father's
weak spot: since I feigned severe cramps he would not challenge my need
to go to the bathroom even though he must have been suspicious about
my long absences.

Somewhere around my tenth year, my father, having recognized his
lack of success in teaching me Hebrew, enrolled me in the West Side
Jewish Center on 86th Street shortly before his colleague Mordecai Kaplan and his followers seceded and started the Society for the Advancement of Judaism. We had Hebrew lessons two afternoons a week and
history on Sunday mornings. Despite the reputation of the school, my
knowledge of Hebrew increased only incrementally though I enjoyed and
made good progress in learning more about Jewish history.

As my Bar-Mitzvah approached, something dramatic had to happen
and my father solved the problem by selecting one of his talented students
with a pleasant personality and a good voice who got me through my
father's minimum agenda: to read the portion of the Law when I was
called up to the Torah; to read my section from the prophet Amos; and to
lead the luncheon guests in saying grace after meals. I met the challenge,
but with no margins to spare. Although I have no gift for languages and
found the learning of foreign languages tedious and uninteresting, my
minimal progress in learning Hebrew must speak not to minor but to
substantial resistance on my part.

The resistance was there and it ran deep. I hadn't a clue about the work
that my father was engaged in. I found the dinner conversations between
his guests and himself for the most part totally beyond my ken; and I
knew and resented my father's negativism toward my consuming interest
in playing ball and following professional baseball. I sensed that his
greatest fear was that his only son would grow up to be a professional
shortstop, not that he knew what the position was and not realizing that I
lacked the talent to earn my livelihood by playing ball.

With the onset of my adolescence my intense interest in baseball
evaporated quickly but my relationship with my father improved only
slightly. He was grieved and feared that I had little or no interest in
matters Jewish or in his work, and that my adherence to tradition was
fragile. As it turned out many of his concerns were justified, others were
not.

Participation in religious ceremonial life either at home or in the synagogue has never exerted a strong pull on me. There is no point to my engaging at this late date in regrets that my limited participation had negative effects on the beliefs, attitudes, and behavior of my children. But one is frequently wiser after the event.

On other fronts, my father's pessimistic extrapolations were unfounded. I became an academic; I came to have a deep appreciation for his work and shared a rich intellectual companionship with him during the last quarter century of his life; and my religious observance aside, I became and have remained continuously involved in matters affecting the welfare of the Jews and the future of Judaism.

A third of a century has passed since my father's death. Since then I have identified four new forces that warrant attention in an assessment of the present state and future prospects of Jews in the United States. The first is the broad movement toward lowering the bars of discrimination, particularly discrimination based on religion, which has been proceeding apace ever since the end of World War II. In my view, the Jews have been the principal beneficiaries of this trend, although Catholics and other minorities also have benefited. Moreover, emphasizing this trend does not imply that either religious prejudice in general or anti-Semitism in particular has been eliminated, nor that the future precludes their recrudescence.

The marked reduction in religious prejudice, reinforced by a great many supporting factors, has enabled Jews to benefit greatly from the long post-World War II surge of the economy. A significant and far-above-average proportion of all Jews today are in the higher educational, occupational, and income levels.

Feminism has begun to affect all sectors of American society and has led many Christian denominations as well as the Jewish Reform and Conservative movements to ordain women. There was no clue to this trend in the early postwar decade when the "feminine mystique" was at its height. Since feminism, as a major reforming force, is no more than a decade and a half old, at most two decades, it has accomplished much and promises to accomplish considerably more in restructuring our society in the decades ahead.

Finally, we must note that striking changes have occurred through the sustained U.S. support for the state of Israel. For many years before and even for some years after President Truman was the first head of state to recognize the new state, in May 1948, both the Department of State and the Department of Defense resisted most requests of Israel for help on the ground that it would impair this country's relationships to the strategically important Arab nations in the area. In 1956 President Dwight Eisenhower addressed the nation on television to force Ben-Gurion to yield all of the land that Israel had captured from the Egyptians. In 1987 the annual combined grants and loans of the United States government to Israel amounted to about $3.5 billion; the Pentagon used Israeli military bases and coordinated with the Israelis on defense plans for the area; former President Ronald Reagan and former Secretary of State George Shultz were strong supporters of the continuing efforts of Shimon Peres, first as prime minister and later as foreign minister, to find an opening for peace. This should be read not as evidence that all sources of friction and conflict between the United States and Israel have been eliminated but only that the relationship is so much improved that it has been able to withstand recurrent strains.

This chapter was written to help the reader understand my background and beliefs before we move into the detailed analyses that follow. In addition it has called attention to some of the complexities of appraising the present situation and future prospects of a vital Judaism in the United States. Even with the good fortune of a unique inheritance, I am aware of the difficulties that waylay analysts who seek to extract the secrets of history and peer into the future. But mine is a more modest goal. I want to tell a personal story in the hope and expectation that it may shed some light on a most complex phenomenon, the future of the Jews in a country such as the United States, which is increasingly open, if not necessarily friendly, to all groups.

3

Columbia University — Six Decades

I always assumed that I would be admitted to Columbia College in the spring of 1927. I had been an uneven student at DeWitt Clinton High School with good marks in English and history but with indifferent grades in mathematics and languages. Nevertheless I made application to no other college.

In the late 1920s, a period of widespread prosperity, Columbia College drew students from a national pool and accepted about 10 percent Jews into its small entrance class of under 500. The Jews from the New York area probably numbered no more than twenty-five. While this restrictive policy was general knowledge, Columbia College explained it not as a measure to restrict the number of Jewish students, but as the inevitable corollary of its national selection system. Harvard College, on the other hand, did not hide the fact that it had a "Jewish quota." I believed at the time, and since, that the Columbia interpretation was less invidious, even though the results were the same. It was and is less hurtful when the establishment takes the trouble to hide rather than to flaunt its anti-Semitism. It is my recollection, nothing more, that the Seven Sister colleges — the elite institutions for women — were even more restrictive in their admissions policies than the Ivy League institutions. My recollection is that the admissions examination for Barnard College in 1931 when my sister was ready to apply was set for a Saturday. That put an early end to her efforts to seek admission. I suspect that my father did not suggest that she explore the possibility of taking the examination on another day because he suspected that she might not score high enough to assure her admission. Hence the Saturday date let her down easily and without loss of face.

Controlled admissions to Columbia College affected more than Jews. The policy applied in varying degrees toward all non-WASP (White,

Anglo-Saxon, Protestant) groups — Irish, Italians, Slavs, and of course blacks. Dependent on private gifts for much of its capital and operating expenditures, Columbia University had an understandable fear of alienating its out-of-state WASP alumni. With the large heterogeneous population of New York City and environs, it would have taken only a few years of a blind-admissions policy to turn Columbia into a predominantly regional college.

But President Nicholas Murray Butler, the long-term head of the university, who had transformed the institution into a leading center of learning, had taken pains not to become indebted to Jewish benefactors. In the late 1920s there was no building on the campus that was named for a Jewish donor. Butler had attracted a small, select group of benefactors, which, incidentally, did not even include the Rockefeller family.

Upton Sinclair is the source of the story that Nicholas Murray Butler in the early 1900s shifted his affiliation from Presbyterian to Episcopalian to assure his ascendancy to the presidency of Columbia. This much is beyond dispute: in 1927 the rector of Trinity Church and the bishop of the Cathedral of St. John the Divine were members of Columbia's Board of Trustees. Moreover, the campus scuttlebutt in the mid-1930s, when I was first appointed to the School of Business faculty, saw the possible successors to Butler limited to Episcopalians.

The tenured faculty at that time was not *Juden-rein*, but one could quickly count those who were of Jewish extraction, and even more quickly those who had any Jewish affiliation. Three of the most distinguished were Franz Boas, the anthropologist; Edwin R. A. Seligman, the economist; and Robert Loeb, the head of the Department of Medicine who had earlier converted. There were a few others scattered through the departments of mathematics, law, and Semitic languages.

I studied with Boas and I attended Seligman's course during the last year that he gave it (1929–30) and later became a close friend of his daughter, Hazel, a fellow graduate student. Although Boas directed much of his research to clarifying the concept of race, I do not recall his ever referring to the Jews in his lectures. I sought his help when I was doing research on my first published article, "Studies in the Economics of the Bible." He gave me a few leads but insisted that he knew little about the subject. At the time I thought he was being coy; in retrospect I believe that I was into a subject beyond his ken.

My relationship to Professor Seligman, his family and friends, which continued until his death in 1939, gave me a window into the wealthy German Jewish community in New York City (and Lake Placid) during the decade when Hitler was undermining and destroying their basic assumptions about themselves as well as endangering the lives of their relatives and friends who were still in Germany.

Seligman, whose nickname on the campus was "God," had served for many years as chairman of the Department of Economics at Columbia, during which time no Jew had been appointed to the department although Jacob Viner had been the runner-up candidate when his colleague J. M. Clark, also from the University of Chicago, was invited and accepted a post at Columbia in the mid-1920s. But Seligman had done much to assist impecunious students, Jewish and others, during his many years as chairman. He was a one-man philanthropic organization.

After his retirement he continued a lively interest in the department and asked me in particular about bright new students. In one discussion about Milton Friedman and Moses Abramovitz, he asked me how the latter spelled his name. I said with a *v*. He was much relieved; he said that was much better than if it were spelled with a *w*! When Abramovitz called on him, the same routine about the *w* and *v* spelling was repeated, but no additional illumination was provided by the professor. Abramovitz, a graduate of Harvard College, returned there to teach in the mid-1930s. During his instructorship, the chairman of the department, H. H. Burbank, called him in to tell him how pleased they all were with his teaching and his research, but Burbank also informed him that he must not expect to be offered a permanent position. That was simply not in the cards. Even Paul Samuelson had to relocate to MIT.

Abramovitz suffered an even ruder rebuff at Columbia. Roswell McCrea, who did double duty as dean of the School of Business and chairman of the Department of Economics, arranged an appointment for him with Dean Virginia Gildersleeve to explore a teaching position at Barnard College. She did not even ask him to sit down but explained in a few brief sentences that the opening was problematic but if anything developed she would let him know. Gildersleeve was an outspoken friend of and propagandist for the Arabs and had few if any Jews on her faculty. Insiders believed that her anti-Semitic prejudices explained the relocation of Archibald Gayer to Queens College, although it was rumored that Gayer had only one Jewish parent.

It would be futile to calibrate the relative height of the barriers blocking the appointment and promotion of Jews among the several units of Columbia University — the university proper, Teachers College, and Barnard — or among the subunits of the university. I have reported elsewhere on the confrontation between President Butler and the Department of History when Salo Baron's chair was first endowed in the 1920s. It took a lot of arm-twisting by the president to get the History Department to accept Baron as a member, just as he had to force the English Department to promote Lionel Trilling. To complete the tale, it was Werner Heisenberg's recommendation that secured an appointment for I. I. Rabi in 1929.

My mentor, friend, and dean, Roswell McCrea, told me that it took him two years to prepare the groundwork to invite Nathan Isaacs from the University of Cincinnati to the Business School as professor of business law, and in that lengthy process he lost out to Harvard, which offered Isaacs a position first. When I received tenure in 1947, I was the first Jew appointed in a school that had passed its thirtieth anniversary.

While the origins of Columbia's School of Business have not been thoroughly researched, much of the initiative appears to have come from leading members of the financial community rather than from the university's administration. Butler's delaying tactics in getting the school established may have been influenced by his desire not to expose himself and the university to possible gifts from Jewish philanthropists.

It is difficult to convey the conservative nature of the campus in the 1920s. A half century after the event, I was told the following story by Aaron de Haas, whose wife, Frances, was the administrative assistant to Dean Courtney Brown of the Graduate School of Business. As a college junior, de Haas had written a lengthy term paper in a course in philosophy in which he had propounded an agnostic view about the existence of God. His instructor forwarded the paper to President Butler, raising the question whether Columbia College should tolerate students with such aberrant views and values. After reading the paper Butler was sufficiently displeased to send de Haas a notification that he would have to appear at a hearing to determine whether he should be expelled. Mr. Justice Brandeis, a close friend of young de Haas's father, Jacob de Haas, wrote President Butler a letter to the effect that he would represent young de Haas at the hearing and he requested that the scheduled date be changed to make it possible for him to come to New York City. The hearing never took place.

There is recurrent discussion in the scientific literature and popular press about whether or not various forms of intelligence tests are biased against minorities, particularly blacks, by virtue of the language they use and the cultural assumptions they make. The answer has been clear to me ever since I took the qualifying examination for entrance to Columbia College early in 1927. We were given a passage dealing with the intricacies of the organizational structure of the Presbyterian church to read, absorb, and comment on. Fortunately I had earlier spent hours as a volunteer in Professor E. L. Thorndike's laboratory where I had honed my skills in reading rapidly and learning to guess, when guessing was the only alternative to failure. Since my admissions test I have always entertained doubts about the objectivity of objective tests.

The most revealing of all my encounters with religious discrimination at Columbia is tied to my application for and receipt of a Cutting Traveling Fellowship in 1933–34. In looking for financial support after my doctorate, I learned about the Cutting Fellowships, only to discover a statement in the *Bulletin* to the effect that preference would be given to applicants whose parents had been born in the United States. I called this phrase to the attention of my teacher and mentor, Harry J. Carman, and indicated that for reasons that we both appreciated I would not apply. Despite his generally laissez-faire stance, he insisted that I fill out the application and leave the rest to him. Hitler had assumed the chancellorship in Berlin in January 1933 and his virulent anti-Semitism had begun to unsettle not only U.S. Jews, but some non-Jews as well. I was never able to trace just how Carman got to Butler or how the university persuaded the Cutting family to change the conditions, but I was awarded a Cutting Fellowship in the spring of 1933. I believed that I received the fellowship largely because of the growing disgust of parts of the U.S. establishment with Hitler and his policies.

The rise of Nazism had a slow but unsettling effect on the rich German Jewish community in New York City, at least as far as I was able to observe and interact with it through my friendship with the Seligman family. I recall a dinner conversation with Professor Seligman in which he stated that he had turned down a request to contribute to the Hebrew University in Jerusalem on a matter of "principle," although he had recently made a sizable gift to one of the newly established Indian universities. He went on to explain that it was an error for Jews to consider themselves a national entity and to develop separatist institutions. I countered with a great many arguments, none of which my teacher accepted.

In 1936 the professor celebrated his seventy-fifth birthday, and his son Eustace Seligman, a senior partner of Sullivan and Cromwell who was married to Maud Jaretzki, the daughter of one of the former managing partners of the firm, held a gala party in his father's honor. I recall that Cornelia Otis Skinner was among the select group of performers. I was introduced to an older lady with a diamond tiara who, when she heard my name, snapped, "Well, if you don't like it here why don't you go to Palestine?" I later learned that she was the senior Mrs. Jaretzki, who had heard secondhand through the Seligmans and others, of my views about the Jews in the United States, Germany, the rest of Europe, and Palestine — views that to her were not only disturbing but intolerable.

For the most part, this upper-class German Jewish group did not favor intermarriage, but they often went to extremes to distance themselves from things Jewish. The Seligman family had been early and staunch supporters of Felix Adler of the Ethical Culture Society. And Eustace Seligman came to play a leading role in assisting White Russians who had escaped after the revolution.

To return to the main theme: the transformation of Columbia University during the decades of the 1930s–80s. I may be inferring too much when I say that the selection of Harry Carman as dean of Columbia College in 1943 marked the turning point. The long depression of the 1930s and the subsequent turmoil engendered by mobilization, war, and later demobilization, went far to lower the discriminatory barriers against the admission of qualified young Jewish men from the New York region. It should be noted in passing, however, that religious and ethnic discrimination against students had earlier been limited primarily to the college and the medical school. The graduate faculties, the backbone of the university, were generally open to all qualified students. There, discrimination centered around appointments to the faculty.

The late Arthur F. Burns told a revealing story of how he was admitted to Columbia College in the early 1920s. His family was living in Bayonne, New Jersey, at the time, having emigrated from Austria some years earlier. When Arthur graduated from high school he joined his father, who was a house painter, but his mother kept pressing him to explore going to college, though neither his mother nor he had a clear perception of what was involved. One day, in response to the continuous importunings of his mother, he took the ferry to Manhattan and made his way to Columbia University. At the information office in Low Library he told the secretary that he would like to talk to the president to find out about going to college. She explained that Dr. Butler had recently left for Europe. Dr. Frank Fackenthal, the long-term secretary of the university and from 1945 to 1948 its acting president, overheard some part of this strange conversation and asked Burns to come over and chat with him. After that conversation, Fackenthal picked up the phone and asked Dean Herbert Hawkes of the college to talk with Burns. The dean was sufficiently impressed to say that he had committed all of his scholarship funds for the coming year but he would be back to Burns in a few days. In the interim he would try to locate some additional money for a scholarship but he could give no assurance that he would succeed. A few days later Hawkes asked Burns to come in; he told him that he was now able to offer him a scholarship; and then walked Burns over to the Admissions Office so that he could be admitted!

World War II represented the watershed. The combination of fifteen years of restricted faculty appointments and promotions from the start of the Great Depression through the end of World War II, the large stream of students who flooded the campus, aided by the GI Bill, and the explosion of new career opportunities in the private and public sectors, both at home and abroad, created a demand for qualified faculty that could be met only if discriminatory barriers were lowered and removed. While Wesley C. Mitchell, the doyen of U.S. economists, had been instrumental in obtaining a professorship at Columbia for Leo Wolman in 1931 and a junior appointment for Joseph Dorfman, it was not until Mitchell's retirement in 1944 that Columbia appointed Arthur F. Burns. In the immediate post-World War II period, the Department of Economics added Abram Bergson, Albert Hirschman, and David Landes, though it was not long before all three migrated to Harvard. The reversal of discriminatory criteria in the appointment process proceeded apace, particularly in the hard sciences and mathematics where agreement based on objective criteria were easier to arrive at.

In his short time as the active head of Columbia (1947–49), Dwight D. Eisenhower was instrumental in introducing a number of administrative changes, which included setting a retirement age for members of the Board of Trustees. As part of that reform, William Paley was added to the board, the fourth Jewish member in the history of the university. The Reverend Gershom Seixas was a member in 1787; Benjamin Cardozo served in 1928; and Arthur H. Sulzberger was elected in 1944.

Despite the fact that during the late 1930s left-wing and Communist activities increased considerably in the New York City area, the small numbers of Jews among undergraduates (the most volatile section of the student body) and the still smaller number of Jews holding teaching positions explain the few members of the Columbia family whom Senator Joseph McCarthy was able to identify correctly or falsely. I knew of no Communists among the tenured faculty and there were no more than two or three who, I suspected, might be members.

During the McCarthy era, in the early 1950s, when many people's pasts were being raked over by the unscrupulous publicity seeker and his unsavory staff, the accusation of Communist party membership was leveled against several individuals who had had or continued to have Columbia connections. What impressed me at the time, and even more in retrospect, was the small, not the large number of persons who were identified. A few additional comments about the disagreeable, in fact disquieting years, when McCarthyism was in control. One evening, on my return from the campus, my wife reported that she had been called on by two agents of the Federal Bureau of Investigation (FBI) who sought to enlist her as an informer. They explained to her that her duties would be easy: to participate in various affairs on the campus and report on individuals who were expressing strange opinions. She told them that she appreciated their trust and confidence in her but this was not the line of work that she contemplated once she was ready to return to the labor market.

During the early-mid 1950s when I was traveling extensively abroad for the Department of State and the Department of the Army, it was disturbing for me to have to explain to the younger and older foreign affairs officers what was happening at home. My congenital optimism led me to assure them that the present troubles were just a passing event and that before long they would be forgotten. Since I had no notion how McCarthyism would be pushed off center stage, this was wishful thinking on my part, nothing more.

I had found several opportunities to communicate with President Eisenhower both by letter and in person about my reading of the deteriorating environment and sought to encourage him to take on the senator, a position that Sherman Adams, his White House Chief of Staff, was pressing. But the president said I was dead wrong: he would not get into a "pissing match" with the senator, for that would only build him up still more once he had got the president into the ring. Eisenhower gave Nixon the assignment of getting the senator out of the way and Nixon accomplished it, thereby earning the president's lasting gratitude and assuring his renomination as vice president.

The years 1967–68 indicated how different the post–World War II world was from the world of the middle 1930s when I had first joined the Columbia faculty. Early in 1967 I learned that S. Y. Agnon, the first Israeli to win the Nobel Prize for literature, would be in New York at the time of the Columbia graduation. Although I knew that the trustees had long since made their selection of honorary-degree recipients, I dropped the president, Grayson Kirk, a note alerting him to Agnon's prospective visit and suggesting that it might be fitting to award him an honorary degree at the graduation ceremonies. He acknowledged my note and told me what I already knew — that the selection process was long over. But he added that he would see what he could do — no promises. A few weeks later he told me that the trustees had approved his special recommendation and that Agnon would be awarded an honorary degree. In fact, he asked me to be his sponsor, an honor that I was pleased to accept. This was the first of only two times that I have attended a Columbia graduation. The second occurred in 1982 when I received an honorary doctorate.

On the night before the ceremonies in 1967, Professor and Mrs. Saul Lieberman hosted a small dinner party. We were at dinner when the first news arrived that the Six Day War had broken out. The next hour or two were not easy to live through, for all who were present had direct and large stakes in the outcome. And no one that evening anticipated the speed and magnitude of the Israeli victory, a victory that marked the high point of public support in the United States and in the rest of the world for what had been a beleaguered Israel, now suddenly revealed to be a significant military power.

As I reflect on the Columbia story, the lowering of the discriminatory barriers followed this sequence: students, faculty, administrators, trustees, and benefactors. While World War II was the first breakthrough, the second was subsequent to the crisis of 1968 when the campus erupted. The reconstruction that followed permanently altered the university. There were several "Jewish" dimensions to the crisis that are worth recounting.

First, the chief ringleader among the Students for a Democratic Society (SDS), Mark Rudd, and some of his principal lieutenants were Jews, which led some of the senior officials of the university to question the liberalization of admissions policies that the university had pursued during the preceding two decades. The student agitators were aided and abetted by "liberal" members of the faculty, many of whom were Jews who had been politically active in the 1930s and who welcomed in middle-age the opportunity to relive their youth. But Michael Sovern, the chairman, and I were squarely in the middle of the original ten-person Executive Committee of the Faculty, which had been elected to assist the trustees in returning the campus to normalcy. The few Jewish members of the board were mostly hard-liners and Lawrence Wein resigned in disgust.

Simon Rifkind, who was an active member of the Cox Commission that Sovern had appointed to investigate the sources of the campus disturbances also proved to be unsympathetic to the unruly students. Both Wein and Rifkind, among others, felt too deeply indebted for the opportunities that the university had opened for them to have much sympathy with the protesting students.

By the time the dust had settled, Grayson Kirk and David Truman were out and Andrew Cordier and later William McGill were in. Many of the stalwarts among the Columbia College alumni had become thoroughly disenchanted with their alma mater during the riots, which forecast a decline in their future contributions to the university whose budget was already seriously out of control.

Cordier, impressed with Sovern's extraordinary contributions to restabilizing the university, appointed him dean of the Law School in 1970, a breakthrough appointment. In my undergraduate years the Law School had two Jewish members on its faculty — Jerome Michael and Milton Handler, a ratio far below the proportion in its student population. And now, in 1970, the Law School had its first Jewish dean. Since that time, many of the senior officials and deans have been or are Jews, including the president, the provost, the executive vice president for academic affairs, and the deans of some of the most important schools, such as medicine, law, business, the college, the graduate faculties, and still other units. What is also noteworthy is that Columbia University's two principal affiliates — Teachers College and Barnard College — have had or now have Jewish presidents: Lawrence Cremin at Teachers College and Ellen Futter at Barnard College. Moreover, Arthur Krim served for several years as chairman of the Columbia Board of Trustees and Arthur Altschul formerly, and Annette Kaplan at this writing, head the Barnard board.

In the aftermath of the crisis of 1968, the trustees agreed to the establishment of an advisory committee of faculty and students to recommend one or more candidates for the presidency. This committee was ready to recommend a Jewish president then at an eastern university when I requested that the committee be reconvened and I be afforded the opportunity to present new information to which I had recently become privy. This request was reluctantly granted and in the ensuing weeks of uncertainty and backtracking, I received a telephone call from one of Columbia's senior trustees, a Jew, who asked whether or not I had become an anti-Semite. He had heard that I was the major source of opposition to the proposed candidate. My intervention, which proved successful, was confirmed by later events. The candidate who did not get the Columbia presidency was appointed to head another Ivy League university where his record proved to be far from outstanding.

The final stages in the removal of long-established barriers against Jews in senior administrative roles can be dated from the selection process that followed the retirement of H. Houston Merritt as dean of the College of Physicians and Surgeons (P&S) in 1970, and the appointment of Michael Sovern as provost in 1979 and as president in 1980.

The search committee for the new dean at P&S was headed by Paul Marks, and the choice of the committee was Howard Hiatt of Harvard. Because of the interlocking relationship between P&S and Presbyterian Hospital, Hiatt had to be interviewed and approved by the then chairman of the board of Presbyterian Hospital, Augustus Long, the long-term head of Texaco. Hiatt went to Florida to be interviewed and, it was reported, some part of the interview was conducted while Long was swimming in his pool. What transpired is a matter of little moment. We know that Hiatt did not become dean and that Marks eventually did. At about the same time, Long stepped down from his post as chairman of the Board of Trustees of Presbyterian Hospital. The board, under Long's extended term as chairman, had acted with extraordinary ineptitude, uninterested in and disdainful of the rapidly changing local community. After all, the hospital continued to provide much free care for the impoverished persons living in the area. The middle-income and working-class white families that had once provided the neighborhood with stability were being rapidly replaced primarily by Hispanics, overwhelmingly Dominicans, many of whom were illegal immigrants, with few if any urban competences and skills. The Presbyterian Hospital trustees believed that they could protect the one thing in which they were interested — the continued successful operation of a tertiary-care hospital to provide superior in-patient care for themselves and their friends. They were slow to realize that they and their rich friends would be increasingly reluctant to use a hospital located in a neighborhood in which the safety of neither patients nor staff could be assured.

How unsafe the environment was, and is, can be deduced from the following. My wife, who was employed in the Office of Projects and Grants of the medical school, was in her office alone late one Friday afternoon when a thief, brandishing a big knife, entered and demanded that she tell him where her purse was. He told her not to look at him, and to assure that she didn't he forced her head down, which caught the corner of the desk and led to the loss of her eye. But the assault was accidental. The following week my wife received all of her credit cards in the mail.

Only since the 1970s have the leaders of the Medical Center begun to realize and act on their perception that for better or worse they are locked into an indissoluble marriage with the local community and that it is the better part of wisdom and valor to develop a more constructive relationship with their neighbors.

Community relations at the main campus also left much to be desired. I recall Mayor John Lindsay at a meeting with the senior administrators urging the university to revise its long-range plans filed with the City Planning Commission, which indicated that Columbia reserved the right to build anywhere between 106th and 120th streets! Questions of money aside, no city or state government would ever agree to dispossess tens and hundreds of settled families. The fact that Columbia owns between 5,000 and 6,000 apartments, mostly on the borders of the Morningside campus — a striking total but still many fewer than the number needed to provide adequate housing for faculty, administrators, and students — assures continuing tension between the university and its neighbors, tension that can be moderated but not eliminated by judicious university policies.

The final stages in the transformation of Columbia from a WASP enclave in the most metropolitan city in the United States to a religiously and ethnic and even racially open institution came with the appointment of Michael Sovern as president in 1980, following the resignation of William McGill after a ten-year incumbency. Sovern, a native of the Bronx, had spent his entire academic career at Columbia, save for a one-year appointment as associate professor of law at the University of Minnesota. His selection as president was noteworthy, not only because he was a Jew, but also because the trustees paid no attention to the fact that he had had several earlier marriages.

In his years in office, Sovern did much to revitalize the university and has demonstrated extraordinary skill as a fund-raiser. His initial goal of raising $400 million was increased midstream to $500 million. What is important in the present context is that Sovern is the first head of Columbia who has targeted much of his fund-raising efforts to Jewish wealth in New York City and that many have responded with great liberality. Earlier, New York University had moved aggressively to tap Jewish wealth and for a time had little competition from its neighbor to the north. It would be stretching the facts only a little to say that from the end of the heyday of Butler's leadership (1929) until the appointment of Sovern in 1980, no president of Columbia had engaged in successful, sustained large-scale money-raising on behalf of the university.

When the Columbia fund-raisers attempted to tap Jewish wealth among the alumni in the New York City area, especially after 1968, they more than once encountered if not a brusque refusal at least major resistance based on the prospective donor's hurtful recollections of how he had been treated during his student years. Conventional wisdom has it that Paul Marks faced this problem in seeking a large gift for the medical school from Armand Hammer, and it attests to Marks's skill that he was able to overcome Hammer's deep resentments.

I recall that in my day the college campus was for all practical purposes divided into the fraternity group (mostly WASPs) and the rest of us. In fact Nicholas McKnight, a member of the dean's staff, and later associate dean, had, as his primary function, the care and supervision of the fraternity group.

Discrimination in the 1920s was not confined to the academic sector alone; it was also deeply entrenched in maintenance and support services. I do not recall ever having seen a black employee until after World War II. The telephone operators, the cleaning staff, the ground maintenance staff, the dining room employees, and security were overwhelmingly Irish. On the other hand, the secretarial, clerical, and library personnel were mostly WASPs.

Further dramatic evidence of how much the campus has changed over the half century are the number of male students (and faculty members) who wear yarmulkas. More significant has been the continuing effort of the Orthodox Jewish contingent among students and faculty to persuade the university to make adjustments in the academic calendar to reduce and avoid the conflicts that involve the High Holy Days and the Feast of Tabernacles in the fall and Passover and Shavuot in the spring. Many different committees have struggled with the calendar problem but no easy answers have been forthcoming. The university has followed the sensible approach of permitting both faculty and students wide latitude in how they deal with the issue of religious holidays. As an undergraduate I had regular classes on Saturday; I attended but did not take notes.

This abbreviated sketch of six decades in the changing role of Jews in every facet of Columbia University must not be seen as an aberration, characteristic only of Columbia. With minor variations, the same transformations occurred at other prestigious institutions of higher learning in the United States from the East Coast to the West Coast.

A brief account would have to note that the two most prestigious scientific institutions, MIT and the California Institute of Technology, have each been headed by a Jew. Of the eight Ivy League institutions, five have had or have Jewish presidents — Dartmouth, Brown, Pennsylvania, Columbia, and Princeton; Yale offered its presidency to a former Jewish refugee from Germany who turned it down; and last time around the Harvard Corporation discussed the availability of one of its Jewish alumni, a leading scholar at a neighboring institution. The University of Chicago has had a Jewish president.

This is clearly a sea-change within a little more than a third of a century. What explains this radical transformation of the academic scene? As a longtime student of human resources I would emphasize the following, of which one or two aspects have been alluded to earlier. In order of descending importance I would note the extraordinary expansion of opportunities for scientific, professional, and managerial personnel that characterized the United States since the outbreak of World War II and specifically since the end of the war. The WASP community was simply not large enough to preempt all of the good new openings. There were too many.

While faculty and administrative university positions never dropped very low on the prestige scale, the world of academe encountered serious competition from corporate life, politics, the professions, international organizations, entrepreneurial opportunities, and still other areas, particularly in the late 1940s and 1950s when academic salaries lagged.

The role of a university president, even at our most prestigious institutions, became more difficult and enervating. There were good reasons for talented individuals to deliberate carefully, before accepting an offer, over whether or not a top academic post would be fulfilling and rewarding. In my view the last incumbent who left an indelible impact on a major university was Robert Hutchins of the University of Chicago, who was appointed in 1929 and resigned in 1951.

The significant number of Jews appointed to prestigious professorships at the nation's leading universities can be explained in much the same terms: there were not enough trained WASPs to preempt all of the desirable professorial positions. The proportion of Jews who had pursued graduate education to the level of the doctorate and beyond was far above their proportion in the population. Moreover, the explosive growth of R&D (research and development) funding in the sciences, where peer judgments play a key role, helped to reduce the scope for subjective criteria in selection and promotion.

We must include the liberalizing influence of the war and its aftermath, which unquestionably helped to reduce the level of religious and ethnic prejudice. When the conviction that consideration of a person's religion in the appointment and promotion process is inappropriate, it takes only one or two unprejudiced persons to help discipline a group that might on occasion prefer to backslide.

My friend Moses Abramovitz, who joined the faculty of Stanford in 1946, has called my attention to another important national force that assisted Jews to enter and advance up the academic ladder in the post-World War II era. For the first time, many institutions in the Midwest and the West were in a strong position to compete with the eastern establishment because of many large new sources of funding. They were determined to attract large numbers of talented individuals. But such individuals were in short supply. One of the successful competitive tactics they employed was to recruit new faculty without reference to their social characteristics.

The growing emphasis on lowering discriminatory barriers against blacks that followed the Supreme Court decision of 1954 also contributed to reducing anti-Semitism on the campus. Facing the much greater difficulties of making room for black students and black faculty, the academic community had less time and energy to nurture its earlier prejudices against Jews and Catholics.

The one group that, as far as I can judge, had litle or no role in the reduction in academic anti-Semitism were the various Jewish community relations agencies such as the American Jewish Committee, the American Jewish Congress, and B'nai B'rith.

This chapter has covered a period of six decades, from the high point in the administration of President Butler to the first decade of Michael Sovern's incumbency. But a narrower vantage can help clarify the major transformations that occurred. Only twenty-nine years separated the appointment of the first Jew to a tenured position in the School of Business faculty and the appointment of a Jewish dean (Boris Yavitz), a native of Stalin's home town, who made his way to the United States via Israel and the United Kingdom.

Another revealing perspective is provided by the contrast between the difficulties that Dr. Butler faced in appointing Salo Baron to the Department of History in the mid-1920s and the enthusiasm manifested in 1986 by the Department of Religion when David Halivni Weiss was appointed as the professor of religion (read Talmud).

Perhaps the most interesting observation about this revolution in higher education — and for the Jews it has been a revolution — is that it occurred in response to national trends with little or no confrontation or conflict on the inside.

One final reflection: I recall several of my close friends warning me in the late 1930s not to assume that I would be able to gain a permanent place on the Columbia faculty. The evidence to the contrary was overwhelming. And I shared their anxieties. Yet I figured that I had nothing to lose by proceeding as if the issue were a nonissue. I enjoyed my work and my collegial relations, and I was accumulating career capital.

I had decided to take a major occupational risk as early as 1934 when my mentor Professor Wesley Mitchell asked whether he should recommend me for an assistant professorship at the University of Wisconsin in the history of economic thought. This was a time when academic openings were exceedingly scarce and Wisconsin was a strong university. But I talked my way out of being recommended by explaining to Professor Mitchell that if I accepted the offer I would have to put my current research aside and prepare for classes — a choice that I knew ran afoul of Mitchell's priorities. I recognized early — and was willing to gamble — that I would be both happier and more productive if I could remain in New York City, preferably at Columbia.

I joined the Business School faculty the following year (1935), but I was not promoted to assistant professor until 1944 when I was on warleave in Washington. For nine years the skeptics were proved right.

When I returned to teaching in the spring of 1946 on a part-time basis, commuting from Washington, I had received no assurance that I would be granted tenure but I must have read the tea leaves correctly, for my permanent appointment came through the following year. What would have happened in the absence of the war is hard to say, but that the war greatly accelerated the removal of discrimination against the appointment of Jews in academe is beyond dispute.

4

Heidelberg University — Prelude to Hitler

For the better part of two centuries, Germans and Jews have struggled to find their place in the modern world and, in their separate searches for identity, independence, and fulfillment, they have interacted repeatedly in the development of science, the arts, and scholarship, to their mutual benefit. The victory of the Nazis led Germany down a path of short-term gains and long-term destruction, which split that country in two. As for the Jews, the Nazis encouraged the majority to flee, killed the remainder, and substantially achieved Hitler's goal to make Germany *Juden-rein*.

We spoke German in my parents' home until the United States entered World War I in the spring of 1917. My mother was of old German stock, a native of Frankfurt, brought up in Berlin with one set of grandparents who had roots in Fürth, on the outskirts of Nuremberg. The story is told that it was customary during the reign of mad Ludwig II for the churches and synagogues in Bavaria to pray for the recovery of the king, but that was not the practice in the Fürth synagogue. The explanation: in Fürth *ist meschugas kein krankheit!* — insanity is no disease.

My mother's family in Frankfurt were members of the *Ausgetreten*, that is, followers of the Hirsch-Breuer neo-Orthodoxy who, with the concurrence of the German government, had succeeded in separating themselves from the rest of the Jewish community and who, among their deviating beliefs and tenets, were aggressively anti-Zionist. During the year I spent as a student at Heidelberg (1928–29) I often visited my mother's relatives in Frankfurt who, though Orthodox, were not members of the Breuer group and were active Zionists.

Near the end of my year in Heidelberg I invited my cousins to visit me. I knew that feeding them would prove troublesome but just how troublesome I had not anticipated. I planned a light supper: juice, eggs, fruit, coffee. But one of my cousins, a physician, insisted that she be present in the kitchen while the eggs were being boiled. In her view one could not be sure, in the absence of direct supervision, that all of the laws governing the preparation of food would be observed if the Gentile maid were left to her own devices. I was unable then, or since, to understand, how the maid could have violated any of the rules in boiling eggs.

In the early 1890s my father had spent a year in Frankfurt at the yeshiva concentrating on subjects that would enable him to be admitted to the university — mathematics, ancient languages, German and French, some science and history. This was not a happy year and he seldom referred to it other than to cast critical aspersions on the narrow-mindedness and sterility of Frankfurt Orthodoxy. When he wanted to pay my mother a compliment he would say that Frankfurt had only two things to commend it — Goethe and my mother.

As I noted earlier my father came away from his academic studies in Germany convinced that the virus of anti-Semitism was deeply embedded in modern Germany. But the relations between Germany and the Jews were deeper than the persistently strong anti-Semitic element in the Germanic tradition dating from Martin Luther and his Catholic predecessors. *Judische Wissenschaft* — to which my father devoted his life — was the creation of Zunz, Steinschneider, and their Berlin colleagues. It was they who in the early 1800s had built a bridge between traditional Judaic studies and modern historical, philosophical, and linguistic scholarship. Even the most rabid anti-German cannot deny this creative contribution of German scholarship to the emergence of modern Jewish scholarship.

An aside: while there are many Israeli jokes at the expense of the "Jeckes" — German Jews, most of whom immigrated to Palestine in the 1930s and received this name by wearing jackets (*Jeckes*) in a society known for its informality — their contribution, particularly to the higher educational establishment in Israel, has been significant far beyond their numbers. The Hebrew University in Jerusalem was largely shaped by the early faculty members who came from Germany and the same is true, though to a lesser extent, of the Haifa Technion. The Haifa Realschule was definitely an import from Germany.

With the advantage of hindsight, it would appear that the savagery of the Nazi attacks on German Jews — which it must be recalled was only a prelude to the attack on all European Jewry — was fueled by the unique role that the Jews had played in shaping and reshaping German *Kultur*. Several points warrant emphasis. France and England were surely not immune to the anti-Semitic virus, witness the Dreyfus case and the writings of the Bloomsbury circle, the movement led by Oswald Mosley, and the behavior of the Petain government during the German occupation of France. But both the British and the French had surmounted their identity crises many centuries earlier and each was secure in its knowledge of who they were and of their place among the national states. But this was not true of Germany which, from Frederick the Great to Kaiser Wilhelm II, was enmeshed in internal turmoil and external tension as it sought to establish itself among the leading empires.

The half million or so German Jews came to play an important role, far beyond their numbers, in shaping the intellectual and cultural life of the Weimar Republic. There are many ways to illustrate this point. One can call attention to the prominent role that German Jews played in the professions, particularly in medicine and the law; the considerable numbers who held important university posts, including physicists, chemists, and biologists of international fame; the leading role of Jews in the arts — including the theater, music, painting; the considerable numbers who held key positions in major enterprises across a broad sector of the economy, particularly in publishing, retailing, and banking. Jews were less prominent in politics and in the leadership of heavy industry, but they were not absent. My mother's cousin Paul Lewy was a long-term member of the Reichstag, a former Communist of whom Lenin had said that Lewy lost his head, but at least he had a head to lose.

There were many reasons for jealousy, unease, and conflict between Germans and Jews. The greatest of the internationalists was a German Jew, Karl Marx, whose Jewishness was not washed away by the baptismal waters with which he had been sprinkled when he was a child. His philosophy and program of revolution was a bone in the throat of all patriotic Germans who saw their destiny in terms of greater military and economic power consolidated behind the kaiser. When that power was put to the test and found wanting in World War I, many Germans could not accept defeat and looked for a scapegoat.

The Jews, most of whom had found the new Weimar Republic acceptable, offered a ready target. And no one provided a better target than Walter Rathenau, who at war's outbreak was the head of the great electrical combine — the AEG — and who later became head of the War Raw Materials Department in the Ministry of War. In May 1921 he joined the government of Karl Wirth as minister of reconstruction and early in 1922 he was appointed foreign minister. Shortly thereafter he signed the treaty with Soviet Russia at Rapallo that ended Germany's diplomatic isolation. In-between his many assignments Rathenau wrote books that emphasized that the old order had definitely passed into history and that the center (to which he belonged) and the left parties (Socialists) needed to work out an accommodation.

I was in Berlin with my parents and sister during our first postwar European visit to relatives, in June 1922, when Rathenau was shot and killed by extremists from the right who hated everything that he and—as they saw it—the Jews stood for: economic power, an international outlook, a preference for democracy over monarchy and tradition, and ties to the left.

Although I was only eleven at the time, I recall the amazement with which I listened to an army colonel, who shared our compartment from Berlin to Wildbad in the Black Forest, tell my father that he had recently returned from an eighteen-month tour of duty in the USSR where he had been training German soldiers. The Germans had been disarmed by the Treaty of Versailles but a few years thereafter they were searching—and had found a way—to escape from some of the restrictions that the Allies had forced them to accept. One defeat was not sufficient to put an end to German militarism.

In the eleven years between Rathenau's murder and Hitler's designation as chancellor, Germany was wracked by an inflation that wiped out most of the middle class; faced the indignity of the Rhineland being occupied by French Senegalese troops; was harassed by the Allies to pay reparations and forbidden to rearm; experienced in the early 1930s a steadily worsening depression with widespread unemployment; and was brought close to political collapse by ever worsening street-brawling between the left and the right.

The ever more extreme propaganda of the Nazis placed the blame for these misfortunes on the Jews. The Nazis found that "blaming the Jews" was good political currency. There were Jews, particularly in Berlin, many of whom had earlier emigrated from Poland and Russia, who had speculated successfully in real estate and currency transactions during the runaway inflation and had become wealthy, while a great many thrifty Germans had been permanently pauperized.

A high proportion of Germans, both among the leadership groups and among the population at large, lost their moorings as a result of Germany's defeat in World War I, the abdication of the kaiser, the inflation, and the new values and styles that mocked long-established patterns of belief and behavior. A basically conservative people accustomed to strong leadership, a respect for authority, and supporters of the doctrine that might makes right, they found themselves increasingly uneasy about developments in the Weimar Republic that did not speak to their innermost needs and desires.

One of the great achievements of modern Germany between the beginning of the nineteenth century and the outbreak of World War I was nurturing a superior university system and research establishment. Only a very few unbaptized Jews had ever been appointed *Ordinarius* (tenured full professor) at one of the major universities such as Berlin, Munich, or

Heidelberg. For reasons that are not altogether clear, a considerable number of Jews, however, had succeeded in becoming tenured professors in the postwar era. I suspect that this development reflected at least in part the desire of the various state ministers of education, who had important roles in the appointment process, to move the political fulcrum to the left. It is even more striking that some of the newly appointed Jewish professors were not native Germans but immigrants who had come from Eastern European countries.

In 1928 my father decided, as noted earlier, to take a sabbatical and spend it in Europe and Palestine. There was no point to my remaining at Columbia for my sophomore year; it made more sense for me to spend the year abroad. My father and I agreed that Heidelberg would be a good choice, but we discovered when I tried to register that summer that the university had a minimum age for admission of eighteen and I had only recently passed my seventeenth birthday. The official in the registrar's office suggested that my father write to the minister of education at Karlsruhe and seek an exception based on the fact that my father had taken his doctorate at Heidelberg and that I would not be a degree candidate. My father wrote and I was admitted.

Before the family scattered, with my parents headed for Jerusalem, my sister for Bristol, England, and I for Heidelberg, my father gave me a letter to his colleague Abraham Shalom Yehuda, an Egyptologist who was living in Heidelberg, pursuing an independent scholarly career. I did not read what my father wrote, but from what Yehuda later told me my father sought his help in orientating me more positively to Judaism and Jewish scholarship. This was no easy letter for my father to write and reflects the depth of his uncertainty, if not anguish, about my underlying attitudes toward the values that were the center of his existence.

The details are obscure but I recall that Yehuda and his wife went out of their way to befriend me; that Yehuda made time to talk with me at length about Jewish issues, and that he gave me the first clear picture of the scope and importance of my father's scholarly contributions. My father's plea for help was answered not niggardly but with great generosity. There is no question that Yehuda helped me to reassess my underlying attitudes.

I had decided that as long as my father was supporting me I had an obligation to observe the dietary laws and the Sabbath as best I could and I followed that practice not only during my two semesters at Heidelberg but also during my spring vacation, which I spent traveling in Italy, from Milan to Palermo and back to Venice. I ate spaghetti *al burro* more times than I want to remember. But the striking events of that trip, related to matters Jewish, came as a result of my running into a British family in Venice whose head, a liberal London rabbi, had no hesitancy in donning his yarmulka and saying his prayers in the corner of the hotel's sitting room. That sort of unselfconscious behavior was new to me.

But it was the trek on Saturday morning to the synagogue that really impressed me. The rabbi accosted one after another person to ask directions and the guides frequently went out of their way in the hope and expectation of earning a tip. But the rabbi after a time would turn his pockets inside out and explain in sign language that he carried no money on the Sabbath, a communication that the guide came to understand, even if the explanation escaped him.

Both the rabbi and I, as visitors, were called to the reading of the Torah and in accordance with local custom we made a pledge of a modest sum to the synagogue. There arrived at our hotel, no more than a half hour after conclusion of the Sabbath, an official who had come to collect our pledges.

To return to Heidelberg: I was careful to select my courses as much with an eye to the quality of the professor as to the subject matter. One of my principal instructors was Eugene Taubler, the great ancient historian, who had been called to Heidelberg from a position at a Swiss university. Taubler, who was married to Selma Stern, a contributor of note to Jewish historiography, later joined the faculty of the Hebrew Union College in Cincinnati. But his years in the United States were not particularly productive. At Heidelberg his lectures were events, in the style of the great master, Theodore Mommsen, who had been his teacher.

Another of my teachers was the well-known economist Emil Lederer, Hungarian by birth, who came to New York from his post at the University of Berlin after Hitler came to power. His assistant at Heidelberg was Jacob Marshak, also of Hungarian background, who became one of the leaders of modern econometrics. Lederer was an economist with broad interests, including the impact of technology on employment, the ways in which Japanese values and culture helped to shape that nation's economy, and the appropriate relations between the market and the state. Upon immigrating to the United States, he joined the Graduate Faculty of the New School for Social Research in New York. Shortly after his arrival I spent an afternoon driving him around Manhattan. I recall that he was most impressed with the divide at 96th Street and Park Avenue. Some of the city's and the nation's wealthiest people lived on Park Avenue below 96th Street; some of the city's poorest lived on Park Avenue north of 96th Street. Lederer had never before encountered so radical a juxtaposition.

In my year at Heidelberg, the rector magnificus was Karl Heinsheimer, a professor of law, a converted Jew. One of my teachers was Walter Jellinek, a star on the Law Faculty. A specialist in international law, son of the famous Georg Jellinek, who had also been on the Law Faculty at

Heidelberg and a grandson of the former chief rabbi of Vienna. It is not clear whether Georg had raised his children in the Christian faith. There was no question that his son, my teacher, had no ties to the Jewish community. The only visible clue of earlier ties was a photogravure of his rabbinical grandfather hanging inconspicuously in the lobby of his home. On one occasion I was invited to dinner, and recall the evening's discussion well because it was so outlandish. The United States was the subject. The professor indicated that he was an admirer of Western movies and wondered whether the area beyond the Hudson was completely pacified or whether the Indians now and again still engaged in raids against the white settlers. It took some persuasion on my part to convince the assembled group that the citizens of Cleveland or Spokane, or places in between, were not subject to periodic attacks, at least not from Indians.

One of the more aggravating traits of many Germans was their exaggerated notions about how well informed they were based on books that they had read about matters outside their ken. It took me some time before I realized that the many misconceptions and distortions about the United States prevalent among educated Germans stemmed from their acquaintance with the muckraking novels of Upton Sinclair and Theodore Dreiser, and the social criticism of F. Scott Fitzgerald, Sinclair Lewis, and others. There was little point in my trying to persuade them that their sources, while not necessarily wrong, were unbalanced. They dismissed me as an apologist, someone unwilling to admit that, aside from money, there was little that the United States could claim as marks of distinction.

These discussions about the lack of culture and the rampant materialism supposedly characteristic of life in the United States appeared to take on an added edge among a people who could not accept their recent defeat and their current political inferiority. They had to find some basis for feeling superior and they did so by striking a claim for their *Kultur*. Let me set the record straight. Heidelberg in the late 1920s had a most distinguished faculty. In addition to those of my teachers identified above, I took a course with Gustav Radbruch, the former minister of justice who had a major shaping influence on the Italian legal system; Otto Dibelius, the distinguished Protestant theologian, who later did not buckle under to the Nazis; Heinrich Rickert, the leading neo-Kantian philosopher of his day who, I regret to say, made his peace with the Nazis; Friedrich Gundolf, reputedly born Gundelfinger, one of the leading interpreters of German and European literature; the philosopher Karl Jaspers, and still others.

Heidelberg University, with its severely restricted finances, had every reason to be proud not only of its illustrious past but of its distinguished present. There were, however, blemishes that were not hidden from view. Philipp Lenard was a Nobel Laureate in physics who made no secret of his support of the Nazis. Rumor had it that he believed Wilhelm Roentgen was a Jew who had stolen the discovery of the X-ray from him. Consequently, he hated all things Jewish. Lenard's fixation was based on two errors: Roentgen was not a Jew, and most physicists are certain that he did not steal the idea of the X-ray from Lenard. But in a world in which the dividing lines among politics, propaganda, and paranoia are often blurred, truth can lose out.

By way of reinforcement, I can offer the following incidents to which I was exposed during my year at Heidelberg. Some time in the winter of 1928–29, Field Marshal Erich Ludendorff came to speak at the major town auditorium, which could accommodate about 2,000. He was sponsored by some fringe political group. The audience that night contained many of the business elite who had driven over from Ludwigshafen and Mannheim, not because they were members or personal backers of the fringe party but because they wanted to pay their respects to one of Germany's two leading generals of World War I (Paul von Hindenburg was the other). They saw some point, how much is difficult to say, in helping Ludendorff maintain his small political following.

I have no detailed recollection of the general's long oration but I distinctly recall that it centered around the knife-in-the-back theme, which all rightist groups used to explain to themselves, and to others, why Germany had lost the war. Further, the general attacked the postwar behavior of the Allies and had harsh things to say about the incumbent German government, but to the best of my recollection did not single out the Jews for special criticism. His oratorical skills were modest; the audience, except for a handful of enthusiasts, was clearly bored by his convoluted arguments but it clapped respectfully at the end, thereby paying homage to a former leader of German militarism.

Several months later, Thomas Mann, on the same platform, read a beautifully crafted address on Sigmund Freud. Once again, the house was packed but this time the university was out in force, faculty and students alike. Mann's central point, as I recall it, was that Freud was not only the gifted investigator of the human psyche, an investigator without equal among the living, but was also a writer of German prose that assured him a position of top rank. Here was Mann, Germany's greatest man of letters, insisting that Freud be recognized as a genius on two counts—intellectual and literary—and that a people who denied him the recognition that was rightly his was diminishing itself. Unlike Marx, Freud had never severed his ties with Judaism and he was an anathema to most people on the right who saw him as the releaser of Eros, which, once set free, threatened to undermine European civilization, a destructive force equal in potency to that of Communism.

The third and last time I attended a function in the town hall, I was not a spectator but a participant. A student group had decided to hold a public meeting to discuss the increasingly contentious issue of whether the government should engage in a rearmament program by authorizing the building of two naval cruisers.

The coalition government was split on this issue and the final decision could still go either way. As speaker after speaker got into the fray, tempers shortened, the arguments became more emotional, and some pushing and shoving had begun among those in the rear. In anticipation of trouble, the police were out in force. My remarks were few and, I still believe, to the point. I stated that it was incomprehensible to an American visitor why the German government was requesting permission from the Allies to discontinue its payments for reparations at the same time that it was considering launching even a modest rearmament program. I then raised the question: Against whom did Germany plan to use these naval forces? That question was the spark that transformed an increasingly tense debate into a brawl. The police had to clear the hall. I did not get an answer, but clearing the hall alerted me for the second time — Ludendorff's appearance had been the first — that even in liberal Baden, militarism might be asleep, but it was not dead.

Some weeks later, the election campaign for officers of the student organization got under way. For a week, possibly two weeks, I had campaign literature thrust in my hands every day by student activists, including members of the small Nazi student group. The first handbill that I read was so outlandish that it seemed incomprehensible, at least to me, that anybody could take it seriously. It used the vilest language and made the most outlandish charges against the left, Jews, Negroes, foreigners — from treason to sexual perversions. Some second sense told me not to throw the handbills away but to save them. I eventually presented my collection to the library of the Jewish Theological Seminary in New York City. By no stretch of the imagination did I contemplate, in the spring of 1929, that Adolf Hitler would be the chancellor of the German Reich in less than four years, and that he and his gutter activists would soon wield absolute power over the German people. I doubt that there was even one individual in the whole of Heidelberg, outside of the few committed Nazis, who would have given the Nazis even a 1 percent chance of success, much less of coming to power within four years.

In retrospect, I have been able to identify a few warning signs. There were relatively few jobs for university graduates in the late 1920s as the German economy began to level off just before it went into steep decline.

The career prospects for many university graduates were bleak. A considerable number of graduates, unable to find jobs, returned to the university to pursue a second doctorate. Many had no more luck the second time round in locating a job or starting out on a career. Some, and eventually many, of the educated unemployed decided that they had nothing to lose by joining the Nazis.

Aside from the independent professions of the law, medicine, architecture, and the technical positions in industry for chemists, engineers, and a few other specialists, most university graduates looked to government for employment, in either a federal or a state ministry or in some suitable sector of the educational establishment. No self-respecting German with a newly minted doctoral degree would consider, as in the United States, of going into his family's business and even fewer contemplated starting business ventures of their own. The acquisition of a doctorate did as much to limit as to expand the individual's occupational opportunities.

Another vignette of student life: Heidelberg and Bonn had the only two chapters of the Saxa Bourosa, the student fraternity to which the kaiser had belonged. While dueling had been outlawed in the Weimar Republic and modest remittances from home had sharply reduced the drinking and social life of most students, the Saxa Bourosa still had a Stammhaus in Heidelberg to which its members repaired for drink, song, and other activities. The premises were off limits to other Germans but straitened economic circumstances had led the fraternity to permit foreigners to visit during specified hours. The drinking bills of the visitors helped to cover the overhead. I went one evening with an American couple, fellow students, and for a time we greatly enjoyed observing the conviviality of the fraternity members, marveling at their capacity to drink beer, and admiring their animated and harmonious singing. But there is a limit to how much beer even a healthy young German can consume without becoming intoxicated. Before long, several of the students, noting the attractiveness of the young American woman in our party, became objectionable and we had to beat a strategic retreat. On the way out, I had an opportunity to look, at least briefly, at the drawings, the poems, and the jokes that covered the walls. Never before or since have I seen such an array of scatological excrescences interspersed with virulent anti-Semitic, anti-Catholic, anti-liberal text. Only an emotionally unbalanced group could find humor in such displays.

But it was not only among the declassed nobility and intellectuals that one could find clues that all was not right with Germany and the Germans. I had rented a room from the widow of a major and she was always called, and called herself, Frau Major. My cousin, who accompanied me from Frankfurt when I looked for accommodations, explained that she never would have rented a room to a Jew but she saw me as an American, probably a rich American, because I did not haggle with her over the rent. The only other person in the establishment was Katie, the good-looking blonde maid whom the Frau Major treated as one belonging to a lower species. Consider this: Katie was under strict instructions not to deal with the nearest greengrocer, who carried good wares at competitive prices, because he was a Catholic. She had to walk, even in the severe cold, several additional blocks to patronize a store owned by a Protestant!

In the same vein: I was wandering around the cemetery one day looking for the gravesite of Friedrich Ebert, the first president of the Weimar Republic. Unable to locate it, I asked an elderly mourner whether she knew where I could find his gravesite. With a flourish mixed with disdain she waved her umbrella in the direction of the lower area, remarking in passing that that's where he was and where he belonged — with the servant people from whom he came!

One more recollection: in the course by Heinrich Rickert on the pre-Socratic philosophers, the professor made a number of allusions to current political issues that resulted in the 200 students frequently stamping in approval or scraping in disapproval. The level of tolerance in Germany for political opinions different from one's own was clearly limited!

I was discomfited also by some of the practices I observed and participated in as a student. I understood that both men and women were for the most part receiving only maintenance allowances from home and that they had little free money for fun and relaxation. But it bothered me that when it came to dividing the bill, the students would work out to the last pfennig what each one's share was. I found it difficult then, and also in retrospect, to explain why this practice unnerved me, but if forced to reach for an explanation, I would point out that I found arithmetic exercises carried to the last decimal point had an antisocial overtone.

Heidelberg brought me face to face for the first time with a small number of Jews who were natives of Palestine, including a daughter of Arthur Ruppin, the Jewish expert on agricultural settlements. They unsettled me because I had never before encountered a group of Jews, young or old, who did not have even one iota of self-consciousness. They just assumed, and acted on the assumption, that they were as good as everybody else, not necessarily better, and they saw no reason to modify their ideas, their speech, or their actions to make themselves more agreeable to the majority.

My last observation about my fellow students: I was struck by the behavior of many of the young women who by dress, demeanor, and speech underscored their "liberation" from what was a staid, conservative, middle-class culture. While Heidelberg was not Berlin, where the breakdown in conventions was flaunted before all residents and visitors, the emancipated female students in Heidelberg provided an early warning that the old society was no longer intact.

As my Heidelberg year came to an end, I had a number of strong reactions and responses as well as some questions and uncertainties. I had been exposed to a number of first-rate scholars, dedicated individuals whose commitment was to knowledge and to truth. I had learned a great deal from them and acquired an intellectual dowry that would help support me throughout all of my later life and study. But I was unsettled by an awareness that academia showed signs of stress and strain, in part a reflection of the deep disagreements about the nation's institutions and goals, in part a reflection of the low levels of tolerance for opinions that differed from one's own. There were professors in the same department who had had an argument about some esoteric matter twenty years earlier who had not spoken to each other since. Most of all, I was unnerved by frequent evidence, in and out of the university, of disdain if not hostility toward all foreigners. And it was clear to me that German Jews were viewed as a group apart, often envied but seldom respected and surely not accepted as full-fledged members of the larger society. But it had been a rich year, with many more positives than negatives.

It would be easy but incorrect for me to report that I came to the end of my studies in Heidelberg aware of the growing instability in Germany on each of her major fronts: political, economic, social. In point of fact I had encountered relatively little evidence that things were bad and that they would soon get much worse. The Socialists, with their allies, were the dominant party in the national government and in several of the states. And nowhere had the extremists of the right or the left gained a dominant political voice. The economy in 1929 was not rosy, but neither was it depressed. Unemployment was high but Germany had an elaborate system of social-security supports to help tide over those who were without jobs.

The danger signs were to be sought and found in the intellectual and social arenas. The loss of the war; the abdication of the kaiser; the decline of the military; the loss of one's life's savings; the new political muscle of Socialists and Catholics; the breakdown of morals; the denigration of the older culture in favor of hyper-modernism—these and other disappointments, pressures, and threats were setting the stage for a leader and a party that promised to restore the values that had been steadily eroded and destroyed. Whether, in the absence of the depression, Hitler would have been able to gain power is problematic. But we do know that the depression and the concomitant large-scale unemployment provided the final push that he needed to reach the top.

Just as I was getting ready to enroll at Heidelberg University in the summer of 1928, Hannah Arendt had completed her studies for her doctorate under Karl Jaspers. Since Arendt dealt at length in her many writings with the origins of totalitarianism, particularly from the vantage of the relations of the Jewish minority in Germany to the majority population among whom they lived, it may be useful to see where she came out. Right or wrong, few students dealt with the subject in greater depth.

Arendt never made any effort to deny her Jewish origins. Much of her intellectual endeavors were directed to finding a synthesis among her ethnic background, her socialist ideology, and her international yearnings. Like her distinguished predecessor Karl Marx, she was convinced that the nation-state was a historical anachronism, which explains at least in part her sharp criticisms of Weizmann's and Ben-Gurion's efforts to obtain statehood for the Jews in Palestine. In the last hectic months before the United Nations acted positively on the establishment of the state of Israel, Arendt put forward the preposterous proposal that Judah Magnus and his small coterie of followers who favored a binational state be authorized to negotiate along this line without specifying their Arab counterparts. Marx believed that the world had to emancipate itself from the Jew (read capitalist) to secure its future. Arendt saw the solution of the Jewish problem as resting with those on the barricades who were fighting to eliminate injustice. Her hero was a little-known, long-forgotten French Zionist, Bernard Lazare, whose credo was "It is the duty of every human being to resist oppression."

Arendt exemplifies the irreconcilable pressures that afflicted one segment of German Jewry, the nonreligious intellectuals who wanted to find a singular answer to all of their problems — their Jewishness, a European identity that would replace German nationalism, and social and economic reforms that would usher in a just and equitable society. As was true of so many talented German thinkers, she had difficulty in distinguishing between the realm of ideas and the realm of politics. German idealism failed her, just as it was a major contributor to the extermination of 6 million Jews, which Arendt, commenting on Eichmann's trial, called "the banality of evil."

There have recently been a growing number of studies that have reviewed the sorry record of the American Jewish and the national leadership's failure to respond effectively to Hitler's extermination policies once their intent and scope had become clear. Despite my deep and continuing interest in all matters affecting the Jews during the war years when I was in constant interaction with senior personnel in the Pentagon as well as with those in the higher levels of the civilian agencies, I rejected out of hand the first reports about the concentration camps. When my close associate, Brigadier General Albert Schwichtenburg of the U.S. Air Force on detail to the surgeon general's office, told me in 1944 what he was learning about the concentration camps, I simply brushed off his reports as gross exaggerations. The concept of mass genocide was beyond my imagination and it was not until the camps had been overrun by the U.S. forces that I realized that the impossible had indeed occurred.

As was true of most American Jews, I avoided as long as I could returning to Germany after the war's end. But in 1951 my work for the U.S. Army required that I visit both Heidelberg and Stuttgart, the headquarters of U.S. Army Forces Europe and the 7th Army, respectively. My wife accompanied me only because I had assured her that we would have nothing to do with the local population but would spend our time solely with the U.S. military. We were picked up in Strassburg by an army car with a sergeant at the wheel and a major as escort and were driven to Heidelberg. We lived on the post and wandered off only twice. One Sunday an army car took us on an excursion to Rotenburg on the Tauber. My wife, who had had no previous exposure to Germany or the Germans, kept muttering evil incantations under her breath that the driver heard and seconded.

I was unsettled myself, but I realized that the young children whom we saw could not be held responsible for the Holocaust and I believed that most adult Germans had not been implicated beyond their silence or possible acquiescence. I hesitated to condemn an entire people, since I did not know how I would have behaved in the face of a brutal regime that silenced all opposition with imprisonment or death. Most Germans eschewed the role of the hero, but I suspect that, under similar circumstances, the same might be true of any other people living under similar circumstances. What remained uncertain and obscure is whether or not there were deeply rooted national characteristics in German history and life that created the opportunities for the rise and success of Hitler and his followers, characteristics that were distinctive and unique to the Germans. I would like to believe that, but I am not sure that I do.

The other time that my wife and I left the military compound was when an army car drove us to the southwest corner of Heidelberg where I had lived during my student days. I knew that the house would still be standing because Secretary of War Henry Stimson had put Heidelberg and Kyoto out of bounds to the U.S. Air Force. I thought I recognized my old living quarters but after repeated tramping through the neighborhood I was unable to locate Kronprinzstrasse 24 and none of the locals whom I accosted was able to help. In frustration we finally returned to headquarters where a helpful sergeant explained that Kronprinzstrasse had been changed to Dantestrasse shortly before the outbreak of the war.

After this visit I reported to General Eisenhower at SHAPE (Supreme Headquarters Allied Powers in Europe) that I was nervous about what was happening in Germany because, in checking the bookstores in Heidelberg and Stuttgart, I found the shelves dealing with politics empty. This suggested that the Germans were undecided about which way they would eventually jump. I had a strong personal reminder that at least some of the new leadership was neurotic. The State Department had had my book *The Labor Leader* translated into German and widely distributed, but the head of the German Trade Union Confederation insisted that it be withdrawn because he said that it painted an unflattering view of him. It was based on the composite leadership of the executive board members of ten U.S. unions!

It was not until the mid-1960s that I made my first nongovernmental visit to Germany. I accepted an invitation of the Metal Workers Union to deliver a paper at their international conference on automation. During the course of the conference I was able to sort out some of my still highly charged feelings and reactions. I met a considerable number of the senior trade union leaders who had fled the country or who had managed to survive their imprisonment in concentration camps. I also met many young persons who could not possibly have been actively involved with the Nazis. In short, here were two groups of Germans composed of anti-Nazis and non-Nazis, a powerful reminder not to overgeneralize and condemn an entire people.

I had another experience at that same conference that unnerved me. A senior official of the Bonn government addressed the group and did so in a highly objectionable manner in which his arrogance sought to cover up for his lack of knowledge, sympathy, and understanding. Moreover, the trade union officialdom were unwilling to debate with him, possibly for good reasons but I suspected because of their exaggerated respect for authority. I challenged him and before I finished I was able to broadcast on German television a stinging critique of the minister's position.

During the 1980s I had occasion to visit Germany yearly in connection with my membership on the Advisory Council of the International Institute of Management in Berlin and because of my consulting activities for a major U.S. multinational company. I could not conceive, even at this late date, of vacationing in Germany. My thoughts and feelings still continue to churn. Many Germans whom I meet and interact with are attractive and able individuals who appear on the surface — and who are probably underneath — no different from the other Western Europeans whom I know and visit from Scandinavia to Italy.

I cannot ignore, however, a nagging feeling that suggests that the Germans may in fact be different. The German press reports widespread and deep negativism toward the large Turkish population that remains in Germany. And on more than one occasion some minor German politician gives vent to some anti-Semitic utterance. But the dominant parties have continued in the Adenauer mode, although with the passage of time the strength of the West German govenment's pro-Israel orientation has weakened.

A Germany divided is a Germany that cannot be at peace with itself. I do not pretend to know whether, when, or how the separation between the two Germanys can be eased and eliminated. But until it is, the recrudescence of German nationalism cannot be ruled out. And a revival of German nationalism is a danger to all, Jews and non-Jews alike, an understanding that appears to be a mainstay of Soviet foreign policy, for which all peoples, including the Germans, should be grateful.

From the vantage of six decades' distance, I look back on my Heidelberg years as having had a formative influence not only on how I think about political economy but also in setting me on a new path in defining my relations to things Jewish. As noted earlier, Yehuda helped me to resolve the last stages of my conflicts with my father and to see him in a new light, not as an un-American anomaly but, rather, as a scholar of international repute. My restiveness with religious conformity was heightened because I found little to admire in the practices of my Orthodox relatives whose literal compliance with the law was far more extreme than what I had known at home.

But no one who was even casually interested in contemporary German politics could have remained oblivious to the existence of a "Jewish problem" even though many of its dimensions were beyond my ability to understand. It did not require the demonic harangues of Hitler to make everybody in Germany aware of the fact that German Jews differed from other Germans although there was no broad agreement as to the nature of such differences or what if anything should be done about them. But on one point all were agreed. The Jews in Germany stood apart from the rest of the society.

5

Washington, D.C.

My first visit to Washington in the early fall of 1933 left an indelible impression on me for two distinct reasons, one embedded in the behavior of the bureaucracy, the other because of a brush with genteel anti-Semitism. I drove into Washington about midnight and found what I later discovered was the Department of Commerce fully illuminated. Practically every office had its lights on. The explanation was soon forthcoming: the National Recovery Administration (NRA) staff was housed in Commerce and many of the staff were working fifteen- and eighteen-hour shifts to get the economy rolling again. Although Washington was my second place of work between the outbreak of World War II and the first year of the Reagan administration — a period of four decades — I never again experienced the dedication and the excitement that prevailed in September of 1933, not even during World War II.

One reason, probably the most important, for the unusual elan that characterized many government offices was the large number of young, enthusiastic, energetic staffers, recent recruits to Washington, who had been assigned important responsibilities, which they had to fulfill within tight time schedules. The reconstruction of the U.S. economy under the NRA was a tremendous challenge, so large and so complex that it should have warned the enthusiasts that attempting too much too quickly was likely to fail. And fail it did, at least in part. When the Supreme Court declared price-fixing by the NRA unconstitutional, it wrote finis to an effort that was already moribund.

Since Washington was a by-station for me during the corporate field studies I was carrying out under the Cutting Traveling Fellowship that I had been awarded by Columbia after receiving my doctorate, I spent my first day listening to testimony presented to several congressional committees. Waiting for the recently opened subway to transport me from the

House to the Senate, I began to chat with a fellow passenger, a southern lady of elegant diction. The conversation got around to the Supreme Court. She told me that despite her conservative political views she admired both Justices Brandeis and Cardozo. At this point she looked straight at me and inquired whether by any chance I was Jewish, to which I replied, "Not by chance, by birth."

In the week or ten days during which I sought to orient myself as to what was happening in Washington before returning to the field where I planned to trade the information I had acquired about current policy directions for past and present experiences of the corporations I intended to visit, I ran into a number of Jews who were playing important roles in the New Deal. I called on Mr. Justice Brandeis, an opportunity that my father had arranged for me via Judge Julian Mack. I had dinner with Benjamin Cohen, who was brought along by a woman economist with prior Columbia linkages who wanted to ascertain whether I was in fact as bright as her New York informants had reported. My former teacher Leo Wolman, who headed the Labor Advisory Board of the NRA, introduced me, among others, to Gerard Swope, a key member of the Industry Advisory Board who smoothed the way for my visits to General Electric and other companies. I also met with Alexander Sachs, the Lehman Brothers economist, who headed the NRA planning staff.

I had a New Yorker's view of the United States, which meant that I had little understanding that there were many Jews who were born, brought up, and educated in such faraway places as the Midwest, the West, and the South. I was therefore surprised to meet so many of them in second-tier positions working mostly on economic and legal issues.

I had been in the field about three months before I got to Washington, during which period I had visited a number of leading corporations in the Northeast and Middle Atlantic states. Before my ten-month hegira came to an end, I visited forty states, spent time with forty large and medium-sized companies, and had had a shorter or longer meeting with approximately 1,000 senior executives. My impression at the time and in retrospect was that I did not encounter ten Jews among those whom I met. I never spent much time reflecting on this fact. The location of the company's headquarters and plants far from centers of Jewish population, their hiring and promotion policies, and the dominant WASP culture foreshadowed the absence of Jews. If one wanted to add some additional factors to explain a situation that required no sophisticated explanation, one could point to the small number of Jews who had pursued engineering in college — the preferred way into a managerial career — and their preference to pursue careers in the professions or in business in which they could be their own boss. I remember the comment that my teacher, John Maurice

Clark, made to me when I talked with him at the end of my field trip. He said, "You must have been very lonely talking with so many people." And right he was.

Let me continue this digression about my field studies in 1933–34 a little longer. I visited among others the campuses of the universities of Chicago, Michigan, and Wisconsin, and in each there was a prominent Jewish economist — Jacob Viner, Isaiah Sharfman, and Selig Perlman. It is hard to recreate the provincialism of these major institutions when commercial air travel was not yet established. I lectured at Ann Arbor about developments in Washington and much of what I reported was beyond the ken of the audience. The frenetic activities of the New Deal and the New Dealers were events outside their experience and, for many, outside their comprehension.

My visit to Chicago centered around Sears and International Harvester. Although Lessing Rosenwald was the chairman of the board of Sears, General Robert E. Wood was the chief executive officer, and it struck me at the time that there were practically no Jews among the senior executives. Before the decade was out, Rosenwald and Wood had become estranged as a consequence of Wood's participation in the America First movement, which was more than Rosenwald was able or willing to condone. International Harvester had survived the deep agricultural depression but just barely. The two highlights of my Chicago visit were the killing of John Dillinger by law enforcement officials who trapped him at a local movie house around the corner from my hotel; and my visit to a physician friend from New York City, attending an American Medical Association convention, who invited me up to his room for lunch, which he had brought along from home because Chicago was in the middle of an amoebic dysentery epidemic!

There are two snapshots of my visit to the West Coast — one involving Los Angeles (L.A.), the other Portland, Oregon. In L.A. I had a letter of introduction to the movie director George Cukor, who invited me to join his party, which included Myrna Loy, to go to a Vladimir Horowitz recital. The hall was only half full, but one must recall that the depression had just begun to lift.

In Portland I became acquainted with one of the young Meiers whose father was currently governor of Oregon and I was invited to the Governor's Mansion for Seder. It was a large family celebration, close to fifty persons. The only Hebrew used in the service was my reading the Four Questions. At the time I was startled at the almost all-English Seder. Today — and for the last many years — my own Seder is largely conducted in English. Times change, opinions change, customs change.

To return to the Washington scene: my economics professor from

Columbia College, Thomas C. Blaisdell, was instrumental in getting me a job offer from Dexter Keezer who headed the staff of the Consumer's Advisory Board in the NRA. The salary was $4,500, two and one-half times my $1,800 fellowship. But I realized, without much introspection, that if I accepted this offer, it would be the end of my Columbia links, since many of my sponsors had gone to considerable trouble to help me get the fellowship.

Although the Nazi propagandists insisted that Roosevelt was a corruption of Rosenberg or some similar Jewish name, the fact is that, with the exception of Samuel Rosenman who had been counsel to Roosevelt when he was governor of New York and who had become the head of his speech-writing staff in Washington, there were no Jews in the immediate entourage of the president. It is important to remember that prior to the first Franklin Roosevelt administration, only one Jew had served in the cabinet. Oscar Straus had been secretary of commerce under Theodore Roosevelt. And with the exception of a few members in the House of Representatives, Jews were conspicuously absent from the legislative branch of the federal government. But both Brandeis and Cardozo were members of the Supreme Court in 1933.

In 1934 Roosevelt appointed his Hyde Park neighbor, Henry Morgenthau, Jr., to be secretary of the treasury, a position of prestige and power even in an administration where the president preferred to operate outside the departmental structure.

In the whole sorry story of United States behavior with respect to the admission of refugees as well as its wartime equivocations about supporting efforts to save Jews in the path of the Nazi juggernaut, it is well to remember that it was Morgenthau who persuaded the president, now and again, to counter or moderate the hostile positions adopted by the State Department, which, to put it bluntly, could not have cared less whether additional thousands or tens of thousands of Jews were saved or sent to the furnaces.

In this encapsulated account of the Jews in high places early in the New Deal, mention must also be made of Felix Frankfurter who, until his appointment to the Supreme Court in 1939 and while still a member of the Harvard Law School faculty, played a critical role as an adviser to the president and various federal agencies. He was a major source of personnel referrals for many new and old-line agencies, and he served as the eyes and ears of Mr. Justice Brandeis who, though sitting on the bench, was nevertheless involved in the formulation of New Deal policy, if once removed. Moreover, Frankfurter saw considerable of the president.

The second Roosevelt administration was strikingly different from the first. With his court-packing scheme defeated (with an assist from Justice

Brandeis), with the sharp recession of 1937–38 seriously weakening the still convalescent economy, and with the isolationists constraining the president from doing much of anything to block Hitler, the administration was not able to lead. If truth be told, with the world about to explode, the United States was so deeply divided that it was practically immobilized. But the German invasion of Poland in September 1939 and the subsequent victories of the German forces in Western Europe enabled the president to regroup his forces. After his reelection in 1940, he was in a better position to resume his leadership role, which was consolidated by the Japanese attack on Pearl Harbor on December 7, 1941.

Within a week after the entrance of the United States into World War II, I joined the executive office of the president in a consultant role to the Committee on Scientific and Specialized Personnel, of which Owen D. Young was the chair. I decided that, if possible, I would tie up the loose ends of the large research project that I had under way at Columbia and finish the spring semester before looking for a full-time position in the government. Robert R. Nathan, the head of the Planning Committee of the War Production Board (WPB), had assembled a group of talented economists. I was offered a senior position at the top of the federal civil service scale ($8,000) but decided instead to join my friend John D. Witten who was chief statistician of the Services of Supply (SOS) and the head of one of the three branches of the Control Division of the commanding general Brehon B. Somervell's office. I had become acquainted with Somervell in 1939–40 through my study of the unemployed when Somervell was WPA (Works Progress Administration) administrator in New York City.

Aside from a substantial difference in initial salary — the SOS could offer me a starting salary of only $5,700 — I realized that I was taking a risk in accepting a job in the Pentagon. But Nathan had ten highly competent economists on his staff. If I joined him, my marginal contribution was certain to be modest. On the other hand, I had learned from my preliminary reconnoitering that the U.S. Army had few economists and still fewer specialists in manpower and personnel. I realized that I might not be able to function effectively in a military environment, but thought it worth a try especially since it was inevitable that decision-making during the war would increasingly be centered in the army and the navy. My mentor, Professor Wesley Mitchell, had urged me, if at all possible, to stay out of uniform. This advice grew out of his own experiences during World War I in Washington: he had concluded that civilian specialists were likely to have greater influence.

In the almost four years that I spent on Somervell's staff and as the senior logistical adviser to the surgeon general of the U.S. Army, I was able to identify only a few Jews in senior positions in or out of uniform in either the army or the navy.

Edward Greenebaum, a distinguished member of the New York bar, was a brigadier general and served as a principal adviser to Robert Patterson, the undersecretary of war. Lewis Strauss achieved admiral's rank in the navy. It is not surprising that few Jews were found among senior military and naval officers. After all, it was a rare Jew who had graduated from West Point or Annapolis, and even if he had, it did not assure advancement to senior rank. My wife's uncle was a West Point graduate, but he became a brigadier general only on his retirement.

Jews played a more prominent role in the civilian sector of the mobilization effort. There was the president's often quoted remark that officials "clear their plans with Sidney," a reference to Sidney Hillman, president of the Amalgamated Clothing Workers and co-director of the Office of War Mobilization. Robert Nathan had performed a major service in convincing the administration that the nation had the resources to set much higher production goals than many, including the military, thought possible. David Ginsberg, while still in his middle twenties, had become the top legal official of the Office of Price Administration (OPA). Isador Lubin, who had earlier become commissioner of labor statistics, played a leading role in the allocation of supplies among the Allies. As the war began to wind down, he was slated to head the Reparations team, but at the last moment, he was designated deputy chief to Edward Pauley, the California oil magnate who got the nod as chief. The president decided that he needed an influential political figure to head the negotiating effort with the Russians and our other allies.

Relatively early in the war, in 1943, critics of the OPA went after David Ginsberg, claiming that he should be in uniform, and before long he, as well as Robert Nathan of the WPB, enlisted. The mounting newspaper attacks, often with anti-Semitic overtones, about government officials of draft age who were not in uniform forced me to think long and hard on the advice that Professor Mitchell had given me to stay, if at all possible, out of uniform. I recognized that at best I might be commissioned a major. But as a major I could not possibly carry on the work that I had been doing first for Somervell and later for the surgeon general. I decided that I would accept the two risks that were involved: the army was becoming increasingly reluctant to ask for the continuing deferment of any physically qualified employee and local draft boards were increasingly unwilling to honor such requests. My luck held.

I was often engaged in high-level and difficult negotiations that affected the power, prestige, and performance of major branches of the army — and on occasion my work took me to the doorstep of the White House.

In 1944 I warned the Bureau of the Budget that the Veterans Administration hospital system was teetering on the verge of collapse and that presidential intervention was urgently required to avoid a major scandal. Despite many difficult assignments I experienced little hostility fueled by anti-Semitism. Criticism, opposition, and objections were frequent responses to the proposals I advanced, but with the two principal exceptions noted below, anti-Semitism was not a factor with which I had to contend.

In 1943 my then boss, General Somervell, decided that the timing was right for him to undertake a major reorganization of the Army Services Forces (formerly the Services of Supply) along functional lines by stripping the senior technical services (Ordnance, Engineers, Medical, Quartermaster, Chemical Warfare, Signal, Transportation) of their power. He believed that this could be accomplished only during a war, and a small group in the Control Division had secret instructions to prepare the staff work required to launch the revolution.

I usually read the *Washington Post* because Cissy Patterson's *Times-Herald* was not only reactionary but also thin on news and analysis. But one morning the *Times-Herald* headline caught my eye — something to the effect that Seven Senior Generals Are to Be Axed! As I began to read the lead column the story unfolded. Harry Hopkins in the White House was accused of masterminding a coup at the top of the army's command structure. General Marshall was to be removed as chief of staff and given command of the troops for the invasion of Europe. Somervell was to succeed him as chief of staff and shortly thereafter the seven trusted generals, heads of the technical services, would be axed. They in turn would be replaced by James P. Mitchell (then head of the Civilian Personnel Division of Army Services Forces, later secretary of labor under President Eisenhower) and Dr. Eli Ginzberg, "two civilians, former students of Felix Frankfurter." Mitchell had not gone to college and my sole contact with Frankfurter had been a half-hour's conversation in 1941, at Brandeis's suggestion, involving the allocation of UJA funds.

The congressman who had provided the background for the story and the newspaper people who wrote it up were after the president, only secondarily after Hopkins and Somervell. Later inquiry disclosed that one of the technical chiefs had got word of the Somervell plan for reorganizing the Army Services Forces and had decided to pull out all the stops to derail it. The afternoon edition of the *Times-Herald* had an even more lurid headline — sixteen generals were scheduled to be removed. The new count added the generals of the nine service commands into which the Zone of the Interior was divided.

By the time I showed up that morning at the Pentagon, I had decided that the only way to ride out the situation was to make a joke of it. I called Jim Mitchell and asked him how he wanted to divide the stars. Next, when someone offered to join my future staff, I went along and suggested that he forward his résumé. But the newspaper's attacks on President Roosevelt and Somervell continued for several days until the president, breaking precedent, called a press conference and insisted that the attacks on Somervell cease — he was out of the country on a critical war mission. FDR also pressed Chairman Andrew Jackson May of the House Military Affairs Committee to silence his irresponsible members.

The Somervell reorganization plan had been approved all the way to the top but Henry Stimpson, the secretary of war, decided to kill it. He was convinced that the existing organization was working well enough not to risk the turmoil that would result from a major reorganization. As time went on, it was clear that I had gained, not lost, by having been implicated. In the Pentagon it was assumed that there must be some truth, if only a little, to any story that broke.

The other episode with a marked anti-Semitic quality occurred early after my relocation to the surgeon general's office. General Bliss, the assistant surgeon general for operations and my immediate boss, had asked me to prepare a plan for specializing the general hospitals in the United States, which had the responsibility for providing definitive medical and surgical treatment for all the seriously injured who would be brought back to America after the invasion of Europe.

Colonel Michael DeBakey, the assistant to General Fred Rankin who was the chief surgical consultant of the army, General Bliss, and I had agreed that since orthopedic injuries would predominate, it made little sense to designate orthopedics as a specialty because all the general hospitals would have to treat such patients. DeBakey returned to his office and informed General Rankin about what we had decided. In minutes my secretary told me that General Rankin was on the phone. His opening comments are still etched in my memory: "Ginzberg, I don't like these New York shyster tricks!" and my retort: "General, you can't talk to me like that," with which I banged down the receiver and stormed off to see General Bliss. I barged into his office without so much as a nod to his secretary or to him. Without taking the time to review what had happened, I said that he had twenty-four hours to get Rankin off my back or I would leave to return to the Control Division on whose roster I was still carried. Bliss assured me that it must be all a mistake; possibly I had misunderstood, but in any case he assured me that Rankin would henceforth keep his distance. There was no need, he said, to concern myself further.

Rankin, a man of short stature with an irascible temper, was a brother-in-law of the Mayos, but he had broken with them and had established his own clinic at Lexington, Kentucky. It was reported that he did six thyroidectomies at one time, moving from one operating suite to the next for the critical phase of the operation. Some weeks after the episode recounted above, Rankin hosted a special party for the distinguished New Orleans surgeon Dr. Alton Ochsner, who was in Washington. Rankin produced the largest, best-tasting Alaskan salmon that I had ever eaten. Only the top command was present, but Rankin had invited me and I had accepted, realizing that it was his way of apologizing for his earlier outburst.

But Rankin went further. When the war wound down and he was about to retire from the army, he came down to say good-bye. I was not in my office, but he left me a note that I cherish. Rankin wrote that I had contributed more than any other individual in the army in World War II to keeping the death toll down.

When I had calmed down after his initial telephone call, I realized that since the surgeon general, Norman Kirk, was an orthopedist, Rankin had good reason to disagree with our decision not to make orthopedics a designated specialty. Further, I realized that when anti-Semitism is part and parcel of a bullying personality, the best approach is to hit back just as hard as possible. It is sad that Jews are often in no position to hit back.

Having mentioned Michael DeBakey, let me add that our work assignments often brought us together and we became good friends. DeBakey was of Lebanese extraction and even in those early days before the state of Israel came into existence, many members of the surgeon general's staff tried to get some vicarious fun by raising Middle Eastern issues in the hope and expectation that Mike and I would have a go at it. But we realized what they were up to and failed to take the bait.

One of the interesting sidelights on life in the Pentagon—at one busy period I ate ninety meals in a row in the cafeteria—was the arrangement to hold abbreviated services on both New Year and Yom Kippur. The judgment was made, and I believe it was sound, that by holding services in the building the "loss of time" by the staff from urgent assignments would be kept to a minimum. My recollection is that the auditorium was crowded.

I earlier noted that Israel Sieff of London had organized a discussion group in Washington, consisting primarily of economists and lawyers, mostly from among those in government service who had an interest in Jewish issues, particularly as they related to the future of Palestine. We used to meet monthly, except during the summer months, and we usually invited a visiting dignitary to start the discussion by asking him to make some informal remarks. I recall that among the leaders of the Yishuv who came were Moshe Shertog (as he was then called — later Sharett) and Eliezar Kaplan, the treasurer of the Jewish Agency.

At one of the meetings that I chaired after Sieff had returned to London, I had invited Robert Szold, a close associate of the Brandeis wing of the Zionist movement, who had traveled by convoy to the Middle East and who had recently returned with firsthand news of how the Jews were faring and the directions of their planning if, as appeared likely, the Axis would soon be defeated. Benjamin Cohen, one of the regulars in the group, introduced me to Ruth Szold, the daughter of the speaker, who was working in the Pentagon, who later came to work for me, and who still later, in 1946, became my wife.

Some of the group had considerable background in Jewish affairs, but all of us were interested and concerned and wanted to do what we could to help work out a constructive solution for Palestine, which we believed would have to absorb many refugees at war's end. The group sponsored the book written by Nathan together with his colleagues Gass and Creamer. It was a first-rate study, analytical as well as policy-oriented, and helped to assure that the Anglo-American Commission, later appointed by the U.S. and U.K. governments to assess the absorptive capacity of Palestine, recommended that 100,000 refugees should be admitted to Palestine.

My first contact with the Department of State came about as a result of my involvement in the second Reparations Conference to which I referred briefly in the opening chapter. Here I shall add a few details about that interesting assignment.

I was appointed by the president as U.S. representative to the Five Power Conference on Non-Repatriable Refugees, a code name for German and Austrian Jews and a few Christian leaders who were unwilling to return to their homelands after the cessation of hostilities. My appointment was favored by the State Department because it would not require them to pay for my services. Through my long-term association with Goldtwaithe Dorr, special adviser to the secretary of war, I had arranged that the army would make me available for this mission and further arranged for a male secretary to accompany me. Dorr, a long-term law partner of Henry Stimson, the secretary of war, called me his "baggy-pants" diplomat friend, a reference to my ill-fitting tweeds.

I also had good connections at State through General John Hildring, the assistant secretary who had oversight over displaced persons and refugees, and his aide, Herbert Fierst. There were two groups in State: the nonregulars who, in addition to Hildring and Fierst, included John Kenneth Galbraith, the head of the German-Austrian desk, who pressed for the conference; and the regulars, who saw little point in the conference, since they doubted that an agreement could be reached. The regulars had learned that neither the British nor the French wanted an early meeting. I decided nonetheless to go to London and give it a try.

Exploratory discussions in London with the British and the representatives of the other countries quickly confirmed that only U.S. muscle could get the conference under way and, more important, could assure that the potential beneficiaries would receive such funds as would eventually become available for distribution. While in London, I met and talked with Ben-Gurion and his aide, Reuven Shiloah, with whom I later became friendly. Ben-Gurion had soured on the Allies, saw them as unfriendly and unhelpful, and questioned whether the Jewish Agency would ever receive any money. I quickly reached the conclusion that the British were unfriendly, since they had other ideas about the money (looking to use it as a down payment of their dues to the International Relief Organization) and were afraid that if the Jewish Agency and the Joint Distribution Committee were the beneficiaries it would put additional pressure on His Majesty's government to issue additional immigration visas for refugees to enter Palestine.

I was sufficiently disturbed by the British stance that I arranged to have the French host the conference in Paris. I was able to do this by appealing to France's long tradition of support for political refugees, reinforced by a recent large U.S. economic grant. The key to my successful negotiations were the Yugoslavs whom I sought out and who were acting as the leader of the Eastern bloc. Once they were assured that I had no intention of having any of the reparation money go to anti-Tito refugees, they were willing to go along with the U.S. proposals.

I took the two Yugoslav delegates and their wives to dinner after signing the agreement that we worked out in Paris and, during the course of the convivial evening, I learned about the extent to which Belgrade and Moscow differed on agricultural and other policy issues. It dawned on me that the Yugoslavs might not be permanently lost to the West — at least that was my deduction from what I heard that evening.

While in London, I had paid several visits to the Foreign Office, as well as to the Colonial Office and the Treasury, and had come away convinced that the British would soon face a dilemma in Palestine where their alternatives would be to send in reinforcements or withdraw. I concluded that they would probably opt for the latter. Benjamin Cohen, who was at the time counselor to the Department of State, was in Paris with Secretary of State James F. Byrnes, and I was able to have a chat with Cohen about what I had picked up. He suggested that I see Dean Acheson, the acting secretary of state, just as soon as I returned home.

I set up an appointment with Acheson and it was, without doubt, the single most disagreeable meeting of my life. He was supercilious in the extreme; he indicated that everything I was reporting was old hat to him (I am sure much was) and he clearly wanted me to come to an end as quickly as possible. He came to life only when I asked him whether the United States had considered what it would do in the Middle East, particularly in Palestine, if the British decided to pull out within a year to eighteen months, as I deduced they would, and if the USSR decided to see what it might be able to pick up on the cheap. I suggested that the United States might start to press for the partition of Palestine as one possible solution. David Niles, one of Truman's special assistants, told me later that Acheson asked for an early meeting with the president to explore the Russian threat and the prospects for partition.

In talking with my father about partition, I had a preview of events still a quarter of a century and more in the future when Menachem Begin and his supporters adopted an intransigent position about the West Bank. My father told me that it was against tradition for any Jew to "trade away" any part of the Holy Land, although he was quick to add that the Jews could entertain accepting "a deal" that might be advanced by one or more of the major powers. But the point that he made and stressed was that no Jew had the right to take the initiative to relinquish a claim to any part of the Holy Land. Interestingly enough, my father-in-law, Robert Szold, whose knowledge of and commitment to tradition were modest, shared my father's strong aversion to discussing partition, much less advocating it.

At one point in May 1947, the United Nations authorized the Bernadotte Mission to oversee a number of territorial and boundary issues between the Jews and their Arab neighbors. Late one evening Max Lowenthal, my father-in-law's former law partner and long-term acquaintance of President Truman, asked if he could consult with me immediately. Although I have always been an early-to-bedder, I told him to come around. He wanted to sound me out on whether I would agree to serve as one of the U.S. members of Bernadotte's team of observers. I had serious questions about the UN effort, I was recently married, and I had only shortly before returned to the campus, but I said that I would accept if the president asked me. For reasons that I never learned, that midnight conversation with Lowenthal ended for me as it had begun, but unfortunately not so for Count Bernadotte, who, it will be recalled, met his death while carrying out his mission. As a participant-observer of the U.S.-Palestine developments, I was impressed with several new developments in Washington. Wilson had listened to Brandeis, but Truman was the first president who could be approached on Zionist issues by Jews who had a claim to his attention: his former partner, Eddie Jacobson; his former staff director of a senatorial committee on railroads, Max Lowenthal; his special assistant for ethnic and minority affairs, David Niles, who was responsible for encouraging rich Jews to make significant contributions to the Truman wing of the Democratic party. One of the major complaints that I repeatedly heard in my discussions with the British government in 1946 was the susceptibility of the White House to Jewish electoral pressures. The State Department regulars voiced similar complaints. One might have assumed that the large U.S. oil companies and other interested groups played no role in the formulation of our foreign policy in the Middle East — only Jews were attempting to persuade the president to override his advisers.

Just a reminder: especially under Secretary James Forrestal, the Pentagon was continuously warning the White House that U.S. policy had to avoid offending the Arabs because the navy was so heavily dependent on Middle East oil. The intensity of the Pentagon's views was reflected in the confrontation between General Marshall and President Truman when Marshall threatened to challenge Truman's bid for reelection if the president sided with those who advocated U.S. support for the establishment of a Jewish state.

The Washington scene changed radically with the election of Eisenhower and the appointment of John Foster Dulles as secretary of state. The McCarthy witch-hunts did not help, since a disproportionate number of Jews in sensitive positions admitted to or were accused of having been Communists. And the Rosenbergs' spying efforts had surely left a bad residue. Moreover, the Jews had been overwhelmingly identified, surely since the first Roosevelt adminstration, with the Democratic party. Except for Arthur F. Burns, a Columbia professor who had been appointed to head the Council of Economic Advisers, there were no Jews on Eisenhower's top team. It is worth reporting the interchange between Eisenhower and Burns at Columbia when Eisenhower offered Burns the council's chairmanship. Burns suggested that Eisenhower might not be acquainted with the following facts: he was an immigrant; he was Jewish; he had been for many years an enrolled Democrat although he had voted for Eisenhower in the election. The president-elect dismissed these considerations as irrelevant.

During his brief incumbency as the president of Columbia, Eisenhower had got to know and admire Professor I. I. Rabi, the Nobel Laureate in physics who, together with his scientific colleagues — Lee Dubridge, George Kistiakowski, James Killian, and others — came to play important roles as members of the president's Scientific Advisory Committee. In fact, Jewish scientists, in particular Robert Oppenheimer at Los Alamos and Rabi — then at the Radiation Lab at MIT — as well as many other Jews at Columbia, Chicago, and Cal Tech had contributed disproportionately to the Manhattan Project, as well as to other priority military and naval missions during World War II.

I had developed an acquaintance with Eisenhower when he was still chief of staff of the U.S. Army in 1946–47 through my friendship with his personal physician, Major General Howard Snyder, the assistant inspector general, medical, with whom I had worked closely in World War II. When Eisenhower came to Columbia he asked me to design a research project — Conservation of Human Resources — to study the U.S. military manpower experience of World War II, which I did and which he took the initiative to get established and funded. He asked me if I could arrange to have General Snyder come to New York to work and live. I was able to have Snyder work as a consultant on a hospital study that I was directing for Governor Thomas E. Dewey, and through Snyder and the dean of the Graduate School of Business, Philip Young, I got to see a fair amount of Eisenhower during his Columbia days. I also spent some time in the summer of 1951 at SHAPE where I was probably a minority of one who advised Eisenhower not to run for the presidency because it was not the easy and attractive position that his friends had outlined. I suggested that there were alternative ways whereby he could influence the American people in the directions he considered important.

During his presidency, I was in continuing contact with Eisenhower both in person and by letter. We had arranged that he would read anything I thought important enough to send through my conduit, General Snyder.

In reporting to the president on my return from my eight-week study mission to Israel in the summer of 1953, he told me about his mixed feelings toward Ben-Gurion. He admired him for his dedication and the skill and the energy with which he pursued his goals. He recalled that he had helped Ben-Gurion obtain access to the displaced persons (DP) camps shortly after the war's end. But he went on to say that he was worried about Ben-Gurion because he was an extremist who might go the whole way, even to war, to achieve his goals.

In 1956, several months before the aborted Sinai campaign, I made a second visit to Israel to take a firsthand reading of the growing tensions in the region. It was becoming clear to many in Washington — in the White House, the Pentagon, and State — that events were moving in the wrong direction and that Nasser was increasingly calling the tune. Before I left, I had a meeting at his home with Bedell Smith, Eisenhower's former chief of staff, who was between jobs, recovering from a recent illness. Smith spoke critically about the current views of both the White House and the State Department about Israel and the Middle East. He was amazed and disappointed that the president was not asking his advice and he told me that he had almost given up on the State Department's ever thinking straight about the Middle East. He believed that the United States was following a no-win policy that would be injurious to Israel.

During my visit to Israel, I had several extended conversations with Ben-Gurion about the steadily rising crisis with Egypt. General Moshe Dayan invited me to a private dinner on the eve of my departure and expressed some strongly held views of his own, as well as those of Israeli intelligence, of probable developments in the area — Nasser would nationalize the Suez Canal; Nuri Said, the prime minister in Iraq, would be assassinated; the pipeline from Iraq to Lebanon would be cut; the only way to prevent the outbreak of war was to convince the United States to take a more active role to stabilize the deteriorating Egyptian-Israeli relationship. I considered these points sufficiently important to cable their essence to the president when I reached Rome the next day. I later learned from General Snyder that the president was also getting upsetting messages from Robert B. Anderson, the former deputy secretary of defense and later secretary of the treasury, concerning his secret meetings with Gamal Abdel Nasser about which I had been apprised in great confidence while I was in Jerusalem. The coincidence of these two reports from the area together with other negative evidence led the president and John Foster Dulles to decide that the United States should no longer consider the loan for the Aswan Dam that had been under study for many months.

When General Snyder heard what I had picked up during my recent visit to Israel, he thought it would be a good idea for me to talk with Allen Dulles who was at the time head of the Central Intelligence Agency (CIA). Snyder made the appointment and I went to McClean to call on Dulles. The discussion was very one-sided: I did most of the talking. Dulles was polite but not engaged. He heard me out; asked a few probing questions, some of which I could answer, others that I could not; and ended the interview by commenting on the fact that he and his staff stayed in close contact with the Israelis. He intimated that he didn't need any help from White House intermediaries.

On the eve of the U.S. presidential election in 1956, the three-nation invasion of Egypt, which coincided with the aggressive USSR actions in Hungary, was considered by Eisenhower as wrong in conception, bad in execution, demeaning of the United States and of himself, and a risk to world peace. There was enough blame to go around so that Ben-Gurion did not bear the full brunt of the president's anger, but Eisenhower felt confirmed in his earlier view that Ben-Gurion was an extremist.

Some who were close to the events believe that had Foster Dulles not been hospitalized when the invasion was launched, he might have passively supported the British-French-Israeli efforts, since it was in the U.S. interest to topple Nasser. But with timid Herbert Hoover, Jr., as acting secretary, there was no possibility of the State Department's adopting such a policy.

General Snyder, who knew of and was sympathetic to my concern and involvement with the Israelis, warned me several times during those difficult days and weeks that Eisenhower was surrounded by friends and advisers, all of whom were unfriendly to Israel. There was no counterweight to their recommendations that the president get tough and hang tough with the Israelis. Although Israel was faced with an ever more strident Egypt that was using terrorists to kill, injure, and unsettle its population, American Jews did not have access to the president, nor did many non-Jewish leaders who were sympathetic to Israel.

It was one of the many unique contributions of Reuven Shiloah, Ben-Gurion's man on Abba Eban's staff, that he was able to work out an approach to the president and his advisers via a leading Jewish attorney, Philip S. Ehrlich, and a leading Jewish businessman, James D. Zellerbach, both from San Francisco. At the same time, Shiloah engaged the support of John McCloy, General Lucius Clay, and other prominent non-Jews in the New York establishment.

Although the friends of Israel began to make their voices heard in and around the White House, Eisenhower stuck to his hard line and forced Ben-Gurion to return all of the Egyptian territory that he had seized and that he was holding in the hope and expectation that Washington would let him keep at least some part of these gains. But Eisenhower insisted that all the conquered territories be returned.

About a decade later, in late 1965, the State Department inquired whether I would be available to undertake a manpower survey of Ethiopia. I agreed because I saw the possibility of visiting Egypt on my way to or from Ethiopia, an opportunity that I did not want to miss. As the date of my departure neared, I suggested that the Department of State cable our embassy in Cairo to inquire whether or not the Egyptians would welcome a visit from me. I offered to consult with them on their manpower problems, of which they had many. Some weeks later I learned that no communication had been sent from Washington to Cairo because a message could go out only if the political desk at State approved it, and my contact suggested that this was highly unlikely, since I was a Jew with known relations to Israel. I persuaded him to ask for political clearance, which was received, and I further persuaded him to inquire of our Cairo embassy whether I would be welcome in Egypt. A speedy reply came back in the affirmative. On the return from my first visit to Addis Ababa, my wife and I spent an interesting week in Cairo where I had extended discussions with high-ranking civilian officials, not so much because of the U.S. State Department's assistance but because it turned out that Deputy Prime Minister Mahmoud Yunis was the father-in-law of one of my Columbia students and I was carrying the photo of his newly born grandchild.

During my visit to Cairo I had an opportunity to meet and talk with a number of younger bureaucrats in various governmental agencies other than the military with which I had no contact. Time and again I was impressed with the nature of their agendas: they were preoccupied with national not international problems, and Israel was far from the center or even the periphery of their concerns. It struck me at the time and I communicated my impressions to some of the Israeli diplomats with whom I stayed in contact that many Cairo officials did not look forward to further hostilities with the Israelis.

Within less than eighteen months the two countries were once again at war but there are historians who believe that Nasser miscalculated and looked forward to a diplomatic not a military victory. But when President Jimmy Carter got Anwar Sadat's signature on the peace treaty with Israel in 1979, I thought back to my discussions in Cairo in 1966.

In 1968 the State Department suggested that I visit the Eastern-bloc countries. All of these countries agreed to my visit, but at the last moment Poland withdrew my visa on the ground that I was pro-Israel. The State Department was annoyed; it called the Polish representative's attention to the fact that I had been received in Cairo. The State Department wanted me to escalate the issue. I refused to do that because I was afraid that it would do the few Jews still remaining in Poland no good and it might cause them harm.

Many months later a friend of mine, and of President Lyndon Johnson, called me to inquire about a conversation that he had had the preceding day with the president who said that he had vetoed the idea of the Vietnam negotiators' meeting in Warsaw because of what "the Poles had done to Eli." He asked if I could fill him in, and for a minute or two I was as much at sea as he was. Then I recalled the cancelation of my visa and I further recalled that President Johnson received a weekly summary of events that the State Department wanted to call to his attention. He must have picked up and remembered a brief reference describing my canceled visa.

During the Johnson presidency a new development occurred. Several high-ranking officials who were Jews became directly involved in the Six Day War, such as the Rostow brothers Walt and Eugene in the White House and in State. Later the president asked Justice Arthur Goldberg to leave the Supreme Court so that he could take over direct negotiations at the United Nations. No longer were Jews barred from having a voice in matters affecting Israel.

The number of Jews caught in the McCarthy dragnet was probably greater, by an order of magnitude, than their numbers on the federal civil service rolls. While this fact was known and remarked upon at the time, it never became the center of attention and was not exploited except by extreme anti-Semites. By the time Senator McCarthy decided to take on Secretary Robert Ten Broeck Stevens and the U.S. Army, more and more of the American public had concluded that the senator was not to be trusted.

The third substantial expansion in the federal bureaucracy occurred in the Kennedy-Johnson era, particularly in connection with the launching of the Great Society programs. Once again, a significant number of Jews were found at or close to the top of the agencies administering these new programs. But once again, I think it is correct to say that their presence was not subject to special comment or criticism.

Reference to the Great Society programs provides me an opportunity to report on how the name was selected. President Johnson had instructed Eric Goldman, on leave from Princeton University and on the White House staff, to assemble a group of advisers to prove that not only Kennedy could attract a group of intellectuals to assist the administration. Our primary assignment, after a meeting with the president, was to come up with a name for the bold new programs that were currently in the process of being drafted. We sat alphabetically around a long table and I found myself next to Paul Freund of the Harvard Law School. The Just Society, the Fair Society, the Humane Society, and still other names were put forward but failed to excite the group. Freund then called attention to a British sociologist who wrote early in the century. I remembered the author and the title: Graham Wallis's *The Great Society*.

By the late 1960s Washington had turned downbeat with the Vietnam War sowing its havoc on every front — military, economic, social. Many civil servants who were eligible for early retirement availed themselves of the excellent benefits that the government offered, and many more looked forward to leaving within a few years when they became eligible.

The substantial numbers of Jews who found their ways into the professoriat in the post-World War II decades had its parallel in the above-average numbers who made it up the bureaucratic ladder in Washington. And in neither instance did their expanded presence call forth special note and even less criticism or hostility. The scope of the nation's religious tolerance had been substantially enlarged.

The Nixon administration saw a further development in this same direction. Henry Kissinger, as secretary of state, played a key role in the disengagement of the Israeli and Egyptian forces after the Yom Kippur War and in establishing the armistice. Earlier, as national security adviser, he had taken some important initiatives in the Middle East.

The Carter presidency saw the U.S. involvement in the Near East reach a new height. President Carter made a major personal investment of prestige, energy, and time in achieving a peace treaty between Israel and Egypt. The outcome of his Camp David negotiations remained problematic until the very end of his visit to Cairo and Jerusalem.

According to William Quandt's well-written and balanced account, *Camp David*, the steps leading up to the signing of the peace treaty in March 1979 were largely the work of the president, aided by Cyrus Vance who made many trips to the Mideast to set the stage for the subsequent successful negotiations. According to Quandt, no U.S. Jewish official played a key role. However, once the treaty had been signed, Carter appointed, first, Robert J. Strauss and, later, Sol Linowitz as special negotiators to explore the next steps in devising an interim structure for the West Bank, which was stalled by the resistance of Menachem Begin.

Carter had won the fight to sell F-15s to the Saudis but not without major objections by the pro-Israel lobby. The AWACS (Advance Warning Air Craft System) battle early in the Reagan administration turned into an ugly event. For the first time in the long and stormy history of U.S.-Israeli relations, the charge was leveled by persons high in the administration that many American Jews opposed the sale even though President Reagan and his senior advisers firmly believed that it would strengthen American interests in the area. Some of the administration's spokesmen suggested that American Jews who opposed the sale placed the security of Israel above the interests of the United States. The charge was the more serious because the Reagan administration was a strong supporter of Israel.

Reagan's secretaries of state, first Alexander Haig and then George Shultz, repeatedly demonstrated their sympathetic understanding and support for a wide range of U.S.-Israeli issues, diplomatic, military, and economic. While there was tension between the secretary of defense and the Israelis early in Reagan's first administration, a better climate came to prevail after the secretary, Caspar Weinberger, visited Israel in 1984.

So much for the changing role of successive U.S. administrations in their attitudes and actions toward the new state of Israel. No longer are questions raised when the counselor of the State Department, a Jewish immigrant born in Bombay, Abram Sofaer, negotiates for the United States with the Israelis in matters involving their spying on this country.

To round out this picture of the changing role of Jews in the federal government, we need call attention to Eisenhower's nomination of Lewis

Strauss as secretary of commerce, whom the Senate refused to confirm; two Jewish secretaries of Health, Education and Welfare, Abraham Ribicoff and Wilbur Cohen; Harold Brown at Defense, Arthur Goldberg at Labor, Henry Kissinger at State; and Philip Klutznick at Commerce, a considerably larger number than the two appointments in the first half of the twentieth century — Oscar Straus and Henry Morgenthau, Jr.

Looking back at my half century of ongoing relations with the federal government in Washington, this is how I see the major contributions and changes in the role of Jews in the political establishment and more particularly as middle- and higher-ranking members of the bureaucracy, which was the arena where I was most heavily engaged.

Without the benefit of statistical data, it is still a safe generalization that from the time of the New Deal until the present, the proportion of Jews in the federal government working in Washington has been considerably above their proportion in the population, not so surprising when one recalls the much higher proportion of the Jewish population located in the Boston-Richmond corridor and the still higher proportion of Jews among college graduates and professional school graduates, the pool from which most middle and senior bureaucrats are drawn.

It is also worth recalling that a relatively large number of Jews found their way to Washington during the New Deal in no small measure because of two reinforcing factors: their opportunities for jobs and careers were still substantially blocked in many sectors of the U.S. economy, such as academe, the corporate world, and many of the professions (engineering, for example). But in addition to these push factors, Roosevelt and the Democratic party that he led were engaged in a major effort both to revive and to reform the economy to which many young Jews were strongly attracted.

The second large inflow occurred at the time of World War II, more in the civilian than in the military sector, more in the newer agencies such as the Office of Strategic Services (OSS) and the Office of War Information (OWI) than in the old-line agencies.

As one would have expected at war's end, many of the older group who had ten or more years of constructive civil service status decided to remain in the federal bureaucracy, while others decided to try their wings in the private sector.

The McCarthy years took a heavy toll from among those who were singled out, justly or unjustly, for being a Communist or having been a Communist. My successor in the surgeon general's office was charged with having a Communist past. My old boss, Major General Raymond Bliss, who was shortly to become the surgeon general of the army asked me to testify, which I would have done even without his having made the request. My friend and successor, Isaac Cogan, under suspicion because of his having been born in the USSR, admitted that as a youth of sixteen he had sold the *Daily Worker* but that was the beginning and end of his involvement. The five-member Pentagon hearing board deliberated for only a few minutes before it reinstated him in his position from which he had been suspended for several months.

Another friend, Margaret Plunkett, whose American lineage was of the best, was summarily suspended from her position in the U.S. embassy in Tel Aviv shortly after John Foster Dulles was appointed secretary of state. She had two marks against her: she had been actively involved in a great many liberal causes; and she did not hide her sympathy and admiration for the new state of Israel and what its leaders were seeking to accomplish. Such unmasked enthusiasm was out of sync with the behavior patterns of U.S. diplomatic staff in the Middle East.

Among the more miserable aspects of the McCarthy witch-hunts was the fact that employees were suspended without their being apprised of the charges against them, and not only their immediate supervisor but even senior officials in their department were cut off from obtaining any information about their cases. My friend, Margaret Plunkett, on reassignment from her permanent position in the Department of Labor, had been in limbo for eight or more months — and, my recollection is, without work or pay — when James P. Mitchell was appointed secretary of labor. I had had a long and close relationship with Mitchell going back to World War II and, although I was warned by many not to intervene, I dropped him a note with a simple request: he should please make a little time to review her file. The next morning she was back at work. Mitchell never said a word to me and I never saw fit to mention the incident to him, not even to thank him.

6

Synagogue and Federation

A word of background as to how I came to write my *Agenda for American Jews*, which Columbia University Press published in 1950. My friend M. H. Blinken, who had played a key role in obtaining the financing for *Palestine: Problem and Promise*, found himself with some modest unexpected funds and suggested that it would be a good idea to engage a number of the leaders of the Jewish community in a critical review of the challenges and opportunities that confronted them. To that end, he thought a small, tightly written monograph might provide the necessary leverage to engage their attention. Without much reflection and with less introspection, I told him that I would try my hand at developing such an agenda, particularly if I could entice my father to enter into an extended dialogue with me. My father proved amenable, as I sensed he would, because he was always pleased to see me involved on the Jewish front, no matter how skeptical he might be of the outcome.

I suspect that I entered into the arrangement with Blinken as much to clarify my own thinking as in the belief and expectation that what I wrote would affect the attitudes and even less the behavior of the leadership. After a decade of active involvement in the Washington scene, I had few illusions left about the potential of ideas to alter the ways in which leaders play the power game.

In constructing the *Agenda* I centered attention on four institutional rubrics: the synagogue; foundations (welfare organizations); defense agencies such as the American Jewish Committee and the B'nai B'rith; and the changes that loomed ahead for American Jewry as a result of the establishment of the state of Israel.

Oversimplified, the *Agenda*, concluded that the weakened position of the synagogue; a shortened form for the thinning out of religious belief and ceremonial observance; the inadequacy of money-raising for eleemosynary purposes as the core of Jewish identification; the frustrations inherent in Jewish defense organizations to alter the attitudes and behavior of the Gentile community toward Jews; and the multiple if largely still unforeseen challenges that the state of Israel would present emphasized that the leadership had a great deal to worry about even if it were largely oblivious of what lay ahead.

Forty years have passed since I first began the task of putting the *Agenda* together, two generations characterized by both continuities and changes, each much affected by transformations in the external environment that determine so greatly the types of lives that American Jews are able to live.

By way of background, we can identify the following important environmental changes. The post-World War II decades in the United States have witnessed the establishment of the most open, least coercive, least discriminatory environment in which any large body of Jews has ever lived. We can put to one side for subsequent inspection and analysis the question whether anti-Semitism has been permanently exorcised or whether it has been bridled in response to the horrors of the Holocaust and the growing tolerance for ethnicity, and subdued by the nation's preoccupation with minority groups that remain on the periphery of American society.

This increased openness of American society to Jews is clearly one important environmental change. If we focus on changes within the Jewish community, we must take account of the following: the continuing thinning out of the Jewish heritage, particularly as it relates to religious observance and ritual conformity; a greatly diminished acquaintance with Yiddish language and culture; little exposure to overt anti-Semitism; limited knowledge of Hebrew and the important texts; and, except for small groups, no experience of living in an organized Jewish community in which the rabbi is scholar, leader, judge.

Coincident with the thinning-out process is the presence of a countertrend, which has resulted in some proportion of recent generations' becoming more "Jewish" than their parents and, on occasion, even their grandparents, in terms of both knowledge and behavior. However, even after allowing for the countertrend, the thinning-out process dominates.

The situation has been complicated by the emergence of the state of Israel and the dominant role it has come to play in the lives of large numbers of American Jews. I have long speculated about what a non-Jew, a confirmed reader of the *New York Times*, the newspaper of record, makes of the detailed reporting of events in and about Israel. Admittedly, the Middle East is an area of considerable importance to the United

States. But even taking this into account, the flow of news and comment about Israel appears disproportionate.

The *New York Times* is first and foremost a paper sold to the upper-income population in New York City and environs, among whom the Jews account for a significant proportion. And many of them, like Jews in other regions, have become involved in the state of Israel, which today commands an ever larger segment of their emotional and philanthropic capital.

A simple thought experiment can help to demonstrate the overriding importance of Israel in the lives of American Jews. Just consider what would provide the ballast and direction to the self-identification and the organized activity of American Jews in the absence of the state of Israel. The odds are overwhelming that we would be a much impoverished community.

For the better part of two millennia, up to the time of the Enlightenment in the eighteenth century, the essential core of Judaism was reflected in the lives that Jews led centered around the two axes of their existence: family and synagogue. While earning a living has always been important, it offered most men and women limited satisfaction and this made them all the more eager to welcome the Sabbath and the holidays when they were freed from toil.

We know that the majority of Jews who immigrated to the United States between the 1880s and the outbreak of World War I — over 2 million — loosened their ties, if they did not sever them, with the synagogue, and most of them found it impractical to remain Sabbath-observers, since they faced the difficulties of supporting themselves and their dependents in a highly competitive economy that gave quarter to nobody. But the loosening of their ties with their religious heritage was not solely a result of overwhelming economic realities. Jews were living in a world in which religious beliefs and practices were being continuously eroded by the inroads made by nationalism, materialism, and science.

I recall from my youth hearing stories of how antireligious Jews held Yom Kippur balls, often within a stone's throw of the neighborhood synagogue, which has led me to wonder whether the disappearance of such hostile behavior is a sign of reconciliation or reflects the accelerating erosion of the religious element in Jewish life. I suspect it is grounded more in the latter than the former.

The early post-World War II years were heralded by a significant number of commentators, Christian and Jewish, as years of religious revival, a perspective often supported by references to questionable data pointing to a growth in attendance at religious services. In the case of the

Jews, there was additional evidence in the substantial building boom of synagogues in the suburbs. In some of the more affluent suburbs the new structures involved expenditures of many millions of dollars and provided seating capacity for between 1,000 and 2,000.

These large suburban synagogues were much more than places of worship. They became the educational, social, and recreational centers for upwardly mobile businessmen and professionals who were eager to participate in religious-ethnic undertakings and to have their families participate in all of the good things that a rapidly growing U.S. economy offered the affluent.

On a more personal note: I have heard my wife relate the story, not once but several times, about her family's relocation to the suburbs in the late 1920s. Robert and Zip Szold, who in the following decade became respectively president of the Zionist Organization of America and of Hadassah, picked Pelham, New York, a suburb without any Jews, as home for themselves and their four daughters. But Robert Szold soon after his relocation became one of the founding members of the Free Synagogue of Westchester (Mount Vernon) with Max Maccoby as its rabbi. And sometime later, circa the early 1930s, the Szold daughters were informed by their parents that they could no longer have a Christmas tree but henceforth they would celebrate Hanukkah.

With the advantage of a lengthened perspective, it is reasonably clear that the post-World War II synagogue-construction boom was not the harbinger of a religious revival, although it doubtless helped to anchor a large number of suburban Jews to the synagogue. Some synagogues succeeded in developing significant educational and cultural programs that further enriched the Jewish dimensions of their congregants' lives. And all of them provided opportunities for Jews to engage in a style of life that paralleled that of their Christian neighbors, thereby contributing to the self-esteem and sense of fuller participation of Jews in American society that had come increasingly to recognize the legitimacy of Judaism and Catholicism as well as Protestantism, giving birth to the ecumenical concept of the Judeo-Christian tradition.

Years ago when I became interested in the subject of occupational choice and wrote *Occupational Choice: An Approach to a General Theory*, which was published by Columbia University Press in 1951, I had the opportunity to study three groups of young men who selected the ministry — Protestant, Catholic, and Jewish — as their life's vocation. Among each of the three groups, the selection was skewed in the direction of young men from lower-income families whose college record was for the most part not distinguished. Whatever other motivations may have been operating, upward social mobility and economic security were important determinants for their selecting the ministry. This is a long way round to explaining that a key factor in assessing the inner and outer life of American Jews must focus on the quality of the rabbinate. In the absence of a large number of charismatic leaders it is not surprising that many urban and suburban synagogues have become survivors, not vital institutions.

The Jewish population today is heavily concentrated in a relatively small number of major metropolitan centers, the most important of which are New York, Los Angeles, Philadelphia, Chicago, Miami, Bergen County (N.J.), and Washington D.C. Close to two-thirds of the total Jewish population live in these areas, and this fact has provided stability for most suburban synagogues, since Jewish families, especially those with children, find it increasingly difficult to raise their offspring in the city proper.

However, many suburban synagogues have been buffeted because of recent demographic developments. Those located in the snow belt experience repeated losses through the retirement and relocation of some of their most involved and generous benefactors. There has been a relocation over the last decades from the Northeast and Midwest to the South and West, which has thinned the Jewish population in the older locations.

Many of the current generation of young adults do not share the values and lifestyles of their parents and grandparents, who were closely tied to their suburban synagogues. It is probably a safe prediction that the period of peak influence of the suburban synagogue has passed, because, among other reasons, attendance at religious services has less attraction for the younger generation of Jews.

If we look behind the data to account for this shift, there are two explanations, one conventional, one not. The conventional explanation points to the ever smaller role that religion plays in our secular society, as reflected in reduced attendance and participation in religious services.

The more subtle explanation calls attention to the large and growing proportion of Jews who pursue scientific and professional careers, including academic careers, which provide not only a great amount of personal stimulation but also a wide array of opportunities for active involvement in professional organizations.

In a career-oriented, competitive society such as characterizes the United States in the last decades of the twentieth century, positive actions are required for younger academics and scientists to become actively affiliated with the Jewish community, synagogal or other. I have long believed that a significant proportion of the children of successful academicians who themselves are often only one or at most two generations removed from their immigrant forebears has had little or no exposure to Jewish religious and communal life. This goes a fair distance to explain their high rate of intermarriage and their nonparticipation in the Jewish community.

A word about my own behavior: I have been, since my marriage in the mid-1940s, a member of a leading Conservative congregation on Manhattan's West Side. My attendance is limited largely to the High Holy Days and my participation is largely in terms of liberal donations. In the almost half century that I have been a member, I was asked only once by one of the three rabbis who have occupied the pulpit to participate in an adult educational effort, to which I responded affirmatively. It would be disingenuous of me to suggest that my low level of participation can be placed at the doorstep of the rabbis who have led the congregation. However, I believe that I would have responded had they made the first move, but I know that the responsibility was mine, not theirs, and that I failed to accept it.

Two related observations: there is no question that Jewish communal activities, including synagogue attendance, have benefitted from the physicians, the lawyers, the accountants, who find it professionally advantageous to be actively involved. On the other hand, there is a disproportionate number of academicians who immerse themselves almost exclusively in their professional associations because they find satisfaction and honorific and material benefits from close and continuing interaction with their professional colleagues.

In recent decades, there have been new organizational developments in the American synagogue. Most synagogues are independent entities chartered under the laws of the state in which they are located; in general, management responsibility is centered in a board of trustees. Among its important duties, the board appoints the rabbi and is responsible for the budget, but few congregations are free-standing. Almost all of them are linked to one of the three major national synagogal associations – Reform, Conservative, or Orthodox. The rabbis in turn belong to an association of like-minded colleagues most of whom are alumni of the same training institution – the Hebrew Union College, the Jewish Theological Seminary, or the yeshiva, with an occasional crossover between training institution and synagogue affiliation. The national organizations with which most congregations are affiliated seek to further certain common activities such as summer camps, the preparation of educational materials, book publications, and national conventions aimed at developing action agendas.

This interlocking between independent synagogues and the national organizations with which they are associated, as well as the affiliations of

their rabbis with their respective rabbinical bodies, has certain consequences. The national associations place considerable constraint on the
freedom of congregations and rabbis alike to design and follow a path of
their own choosing. The three major divisions — four if the Reconstructionist movement is included — must rule with a light hand if they want to
attract and retain the allegiance of their graduates. Nevertheless, each
national organization of rabbis and congregations has a set of articulated
positions about thought and practice, which its adherents are expected to
acknowledge and respect. Since a career in the rabbinate often involves
moving from a smaller to a larger congregation, the national rabbinical
organizations that oversee the placement of rabbis exercise a considerable, if indirect, influence on the behavior of their members. While the
older, well-established members of the rabbinate do not need the assistance of the placement office to locate a position or guidance in negotiating their salary or fringe benefits, recent graduates do. The latter soon
learn how the game is played and most tend to conform to the rules.

The wide range in beliefs and practices among the congregations and
rabbis associated with each of the respective national organizations reflects the desire of the national bodies to maintain the allegiance and
active involvement of the maximum number of like-minded synagogues
and rabbis. Any attempt by the national leadership to insist on a narrow
set of beliefs and practices would inevitably lead to withdrawals and
resignations and the emergence of competing groups. Even the Orthodox, who have less scope for temporizing in matters of belief and practice, have gone a fair distance not to lean too heavily on congregations
whose practices are borderline and sometimes beyond what the national
leadership prefers.

While it is still easy to distinguish between the right wing of the Conservative movement and the left wing of Reform, in both beliefs and
practices, this is no longer true for many congregations that occupy the
middle ground. First, only a small minority of individuals associated
with Conservative congregations are Sabbath observers, follow the dietary laws, or otherwise live in accordance with traditional obligations.
They may be more "observant" on average than their counterparts in
Reform congregations, but the measuring instrument is calibrated not to
Halachah but to peripheral aspects of observance.

Now that the Conservative movement has joined the Reform in ordain-
ing women as rabbis, the principal doctrinal issue that continues to separate the two movements relates to the conditions under which their affiliated rabbis will conduct a marriage in which only one of the parties is a
Jew, defined as an offspring of a Jewish mother.

Just as all private U.S. universities are heavily dependent on their alumni for annual financial contributions, as well as for donations to capital campaigns, the same holds for the Hebrew Union College (HUC) and the Jewish Theological Seminary (JTS). This symbolic relationship affected HUC much earlier than JTS, but today both institutions look to their alumni and the congregations they lead for much of the financing they need to carry out their educational, research, and organizational roles.

Clearly, financial dependency has an effect on the attitudes and behavior of the leadership and faculties of these institutions. From time to time they may see their challenges and opportunities as somewhat different, and occasionally as strikingly different, from how their alumni see them. But the flagship institutions cannot act independently. They need the continuing wholehearted support of their alumni. They cannot afford to lose their good will.

I recall a discussion shortly after the end of World War II with Louis Finkelstein, the long-term chancellor of JTS, in which he remarked on the much narrower degree of freedom facing his counterpart in Cincinnati. The graduates of HUC played a much more prominent role in the direction of their alma mater than did the graduates of the seminary. Dr. Finkelstein explained that he hoped to be able to obtain the bulk of the seminary's financing from sources other than its alumni because, among other reasons, he would thereby have more freedom in pursuing the academic and research goals that were high on his agenda.

One of Finkelstein's early agenda items was the establishment of the Conference on Science, Philosophy, and Religion in association with two Columbia professors, Robert M. MacIver and Lyman Bryson. This was one of the first if not *the* first major undertaking that sought to flesh out the new "ecumenicalism" with representatives from the three major faiths, and with philosophers, social scientists, and natural scientists added to enlarge the effort beyond the purely theological arena.

I was asked to contribute papers from an economic perspective to many of the annual conferences' themes, which I accepted because I found that the discussions forced me to consider problems beyond my discipline's ken that I found interesting and on occasion even exciting. In retrospect I would, however, be hard pressed to identify any concrete, constructive result that emerged from a decade or more of these conferences. But many of the other participants — who like myself were repeaters — may have found the annual engagement personally rewarding and let it go at that.

My general impression is that the differences between HUC and JTS in the roles played by their alumni in the late 1940s have been substantially narrowed with JTS becoming more dependent on its graduates for ongoing financial support, which in turn has enabled them to exercise more influence on the direction of the institution.

Although there are a number of Reform, Conservative, and even a few Orthodox rabbis who have been recognized as important leaders in their local communities and occasionally even in their region, at present there is not a single rabbi of national visibility and fame. One explanation is the heavy work load that encumbers the successful rabbi in looking after his large congregation and participating in the range of local activities that demand his attention.

Another explanation would call attention to the long-term tension between rabbinic and lay leadership in national organizations, a tension that dates back to the beginning of this century with the organization of the American Jewish Committee (AJC). From the days of Jacob Schiff and Louis Marshall, the leaders of the AJC saw little point in sharing power with members of the rabbinate, particularly since they did not believe that oratorical skills and public presence could compete with behind-the-scenes negotiations and persuasion in furthering Jewish objectives. The American Jewish Congress, alone among the larger national organizations, was led in the postwar period over a long stretch of years by a rabbi, Arthur Hertzberg.

The synagogue provided the historic base for organizing Jewish life. But with a large number of American Jews, indifferent if not hostile to organized religion and with a considerable number of them balking at formally affiliating with a congregation, there had long been a need for alternative structures and the local federation early came to fill the gap. The federation became the principal fund-raising arm for the support of local institutions, a limited number of national institutions that have been placed on a short list, and the major conduit for the United Jewish Appeal, which funnels funds to Israel and to a few other agencies such as the Joint Distribution Committee that assists Jews not only in Israel but in the Diaspora.

The relatively large amounts of money that the federations are able to obtain annually from the local Jews, circa $777 million in 1987, reflect the following: a well-organized, professionally led campaign organization in which large numbers of volunteers play leading roles; in New York City and in many other large communities the dominant pattern is organized by industry; emphasis is placed on eliciting an initial number of large gifts within each sector to set the stage for informed volunteers to explain to each of their prospects the size of their appropriate gift in light of the sums that have already been pledged and the goals that must be met. The presumption is that the leaders in the several branches are well informed about the earnings of the business people whom they approach, and that they are in a good position to shame, threaten, or bully reluctant contributors to raise their pledges.

Despite this finely honed structure with its admixture of skilled professionals and dedicated volunteers, it should be emphasized that in the largest Jewish communities, such as those in New York, Los Angeles, and Chicago, only a minority of potential donors participate in the annual campaign. The large federations are still heavily dependent on large gifts from a relatively small number of contributors. About one-quarter to one-third of all Jews contribute annually; and the predominant sums are contributed by about one in ten of the contributors.

The participation rate is considerably greater in smaller, well-organized communities where a much higher proportion of all Jews are affiliated with Jewish activities from the synagogue to the country club and where powerful community pressure can be exerted to ensure that everybody capable of contributing does so.

Much of the original impetus for the establishment and strengthening of local federations came from the desire of the lay leaders to simplify the costly and duplicative efforts among dozens of voluntary health, social welfare, educational, and community organizations seeking the dollars they needed for their annual operations by mounting individual fund-raising campaigns.

Once the federations were in a position to guarantee the several agencies a level of annual support that would not be less than they had been able to secure on their own, permitted them to seek capital funding on their own, and held forth the promise of raising more money in the future to be distributed among the participating agencies, the scene was set for the strong growth of the federation movement.

In its long formative period, that is, up to World War II, the federation leadership was largely under the control of German Jewish leaders, who also tended to be among the more wealthy members of the community. These Jews sought to play a role in local Jewish affairs that would not involve them in religious or ideological conflicts and that could broaden and deepen their social life at a time when the Christian elite were unwilling to welcome them into their organizations.

Since many among this German Jewish leadership were hesitant about becoming too deeply involved in Jewish affairs, participating in their local federation offered a happy compromise. They had few qualms about contributing to and soliciting contributions for hospitals, child-care agencies, old-age homes, psychiatric and counseling services, and other philanthropic endeavors. The early federations for the most part showed little sensitivity for Jewish tradition and ceremonials. Customarily they served nonkosher food at their functions.

Federations followed conservative allocation principles. Most large member agencies received roughly the same absolute and/or relative percentage of the total in a given year as they had in the previous year. Once the federation was well established, it was difficult for new agencies to gain admission. The leadership wanted assurances that the new agencies would increase the inflow of contributions to cover their allocation and to leave a little over for distribution to the established agencies.

Major transformations have occurred in the federation structure and operations since the outbreak of World War II. The major fund-raising agencies for assisting Jews in Palestine and in other overseas areas—the United Palestine Appeal and the Joint Distribution Committee—got together in 1940 and established the United Jewish Appeal (UJA). This new instrumentality, aided by the growing affluence of Jews during and after the war, was able to achieve ever higher levels of contributions. Each previous goal was exceeded as successive crises arose, such as the challenge of resettling the survivors of the DP camps; helping the new state of Israel absorb several hundred thousand emigrants from Muslim countries; the aftermath of the Sinai campaign; the Six Day War; the resettlement of emigrants from the USSR; the Yom Kippur War; and other less momentous happenings, all of which could be eased—if not resolved—by larger donations from the only large, affluent, concerned Jewish community in the Diaspora.

For many years the distribution of the funds raised by the fully integrated federations—until recently New York City held separate campaigns for local and overseas purposes—were divided roughly as follows: about 55 percent for overseas relief and rehabilitation, mostly in Israel; close to 40 percent for the support of local institutions; the remainder for a small number of national Jewish organizations such as the American Jewish Historical Association, YIVO, (Yïddishe Visenschafliche Organization) and so forth.

Over the years the Israelis worked out special arrangements with the United Jewish Appeal that enabled them to pursue supplemental efforts at fund-raising, including in particular the sale of Israeli bonds. Provision was also made for separate campaigns for the major institutions of higher learning in Israel such as the Hebrew University, the Weizmann Institute, the Technion, and others, and for Hadassah to continue its independent fund-raising activities.

While there are acrimonious discussions from time to time about whether or not the spirit as well as the terms of extant agreements concerning fund-raising are being fully observed by all parties, the basic framework laid down for the UJA fifty years ago has held with only minor modifications.

In addition to this formal structure of fund-raising, the several sectors of the Orthodox community in the United States have become increasingly important contributors to the support of yeshivas and other religious-educational-social welfare institutions in Israel.

The Orthodox are not alone in having targeted certain important activities in Israel and in funding them. So have a number of Israeli-based efforts, primarily in the cultural and artistic fields, which have established groups of friends in the United States to assist in financing. And there are a number of private and community-based foundations in the United States, some dating back to the 1920s, that continue to forward funds to Israel for designated philanthropic purposes.

This complicated flow of philanthropic funds from the United States to Israel has led on occasion to discussions, even public challenges, about the logic and justification for such large overseas disbursements. Some critics have questioned whether retaining larger sums to strengthen the Jewish infrastructure in America might not yield greater benefits to American Jews and, over time, to the Israelis as well, who will have to rely for many years to come on a flourishing and involved Jewish community in the United States. But this suggested approach never made much headway because the proponents could not demonstrate how the Israelis could get through their recurrent fiscal crises with less money from American Jewry.

The allocation of UJA monies has also been challenged by many activists on behalf of Israel who point to the fact that the greatly enlarged total contributions reflect primarily the concerns of American Jews to the recurrent crises that the new state has confronted over its short life. In the opinion of these activists it is questionable that a reduced flow of funds to Israel would lead to more monies becoming available for local and national objectives within the United States. In their view if less money were allocated to Israel, the total level of giving would decline.

There are additional points about the flow of funds from American Jews to Israel that should at least be briefly noted. A few Israelis, outside the establishment, believe that the liberal flow of funds from American Jews has led to excessive bureaucratization and politicization of the Jewish Agency, which oversees the distribution of most of these funds. Since there is an overlap between the political parties in Israel and the Jewish Agency, some critics believe that the distribution of these large sums from American Jews has had a negative effect on the Israeli political environment. This has made it relatively easy for the in-groups to strengthen themselves and to stifle potential opposition.

Ever since the invasion of Lebanon in 1982, an increasing number of concerned American Jews have questioned whether they want to see the funds they contribute remain under the control of political groups in Israel whose policies — such as the settlement of the West Bank — they strenuously oppose. Some have found other conduits through which to forward their contributions to Israel, although it is difficult to estimate the extent of this deflection.

Long before the invasion of Lebanon, the issue surfaced of American Jews' playing a more active role in the distribution of their philanthropic gifts to Israel. But it turned out that the issue was easier to raise than to solve. The Israeli leadership took the position that only those willing to live in Israel and share the responsibility for defending the nation could play a role in the shaping of policy. Moreover, only a small minority of American Jewish leaders were willing to contemplate getting so deeply involved in Israeli affairs that they would be in a position to make informed judgments about alternative uses of the philanthropic funds from the United States. It was more or less inevitable therefore that the Israeli leadership would continue to make the critical decisions about how these funds would be used.

At one point, the United States government became involved. The Internal Revenue Service (IRS) sets conditions governing the tax deductibility of funds sent abroad. It raised questions about whether or not some of the contributions were used for purposes that did not conform to its specifications. Dr. Isador Lubin was appointed and served for a period of years as the head of a small office whose responsibility it was to monitor the uses to which U.S. philanthropic contributions were put to assure compliance with the regulations of the IRS.

Another aspect of American Jewish life relates to the changing nature of the leadership. The dominance of the old German Jewish families has definitely receded. More and more of the large givers, who are also the current leaders, are of East European background, and many of them are more positive about their Jewish identification and respect tradition and ritual.

This shift in leadership has gone hand in hand with the growing appreciation of the importance of Jewish education for the survival and vitality of the American Jewish community, and this has led most federations to increase their support for local Jewish educational activities.

Because of their heavy commitments to their local health and social welfare agencies and the continuing demands on them for increased contributions to Israel, most federations have experienced difficulties in increasing their support for Jewish education as quickly as they might have preferred. But they are doing much more than in the past on the educational front.

Federations face additional difficulties in their efforts to broaden and deepen their support for Jewish education. They run into conflicts with congregations that have long operated religious schools. They have found it next to impossible to persuade congregations in the same area to rationalize their educational efforts by joining together to run a larger but more effective school system. And they face difficulties in establishing sliding scales of tuition to assist lower-income parents whose children are enrolled in religious day schools.

In recent years the Council of Jewish Federations has emphasized its planning and budgeting activities and has viewed its annual assemblies as the major national effort to look critically at the changing agenda confronting American Jews. But the record does not reveal results commensurate with these ambitious objectives. The past continues to limit the degrees of freedom allotted to the budget-makers. For the reasons just identified, federations are constrained in their efforts to strengthen the extant Jewish educational system, which everyone acknowledges requires improvement.

The synagogue and the federation are the principal centers of Jewish affiliation, although observers have different views of their respective strengths and weaknesses. More difficulty attaches to appraising the roles of the three long-established national Jewish defense organizations — the B'nai B'rith Anti-Defamation League, the American Jewish Committee, and the American Jewish Congress. One could argue that the emergence of the state of Israel and its continuing need for assistance from American Jews — financial, political leverage, and public relations — has preempted the American Jewish stage. In the post-World War II decades both the B'nai B'rith and the AJC, which in earlier times had kept their distance from Zionism, are no longer aloof, and when Israel is in need they are supportive.

It could also be argued that the emergence of the state of Israel has tended, if only by indirection, to move the B'nai B'rith and the AJC away from their pre-World War II preoccupation with "defense" activities to a more positive, constructive orientation aimed at strengthening the internal American Jewish community. In the late 1920s B'nai B'rith started to play a leading role in establishing Hillel chapters at various colleges and universities. This effort proved so successful that the financing became more than its local lodges could continue underwriting, with the result that local federations increasingly assumed the role of financial sponsors.

While the three defense organizations have continued to monitor and respond to anti-Semitic activities, the last decades have seen some reduction in these activities, surely in comparison to the volatile 1920s and 1930s. The AJC, for example, in particular, has underwritten research and educational programs directed to deepening its own and the nation's understanding of the institutional framework for religious liberty and the rights of minorities. Further, it has initiated a number of joint cultural projects with non-Jewish organizations that share its philosophical and political orientations.

Shortly after the end of World War II the three major defense organizations together with the fourth that was solely focused on intergroup relations — the National Community Relations Advisory Council — invited the distinguished Columbia University sociologist Robert Morrison MacIver to study their organizational structures and their respective agendas with an aim of recommending how duplications and overlapping might be reduced. MacIver, who had been my teacher and who was a close personal friend, explored with me the pros and cons of accepting this assignment. Although I was not privy to all or even most of the infighting among the agencies, I knew enough about their bureaucratization to raise serious questions about MacIver's accepting their offer. I feared that no matter how sensible his recommendations, they would not be implemented. MacIver took on the task, worked hard at it, but his report was never given a fair hearing. In fact he was so shabbily treated by the parties that I found an occasion to criticize his critics and to offer him a public apology for their unseemly behavior.

The last quarter century has witnessed the coming of age of the ecumenical movement. I can offer the following illustration. In 1959 I served as the chairman of studies for the Golden Anniversary White House Conference on Children and Youth. My fellow members on the Executive Committee made it clear that one of my assignments was to have organized religion contribute to the preparation of background papers. They suggested that I elicit essays from each of the three major faiths. I thought this was a poor way to proceed and recommended instead that the representatives of the three faiths submit a single paper setting forth their shared views and recommendations. There was no problem in obtaining agreement from the Protestant and Jewish representatives, who were pleased to cooperate, but the Catholic monsigneur did not see how he could join them. On the basis of discussions that I had earlier had in Rome, I suggested that he inquire of the Vatican whether he could collaborate or not. He was dubious about following my suggestion but decided to try it. To the best of my knowledge the first ecumenical article on religion published in the United States signed by representatives of the three major faiths was the chapter prepared for *The Nation's Children* (Columbia University Press, 1960).

The expanded Jewish-Christian ecumenical efforts, in which the AJC played a leading role, unquestionably contributed to the decision of Vatican Council II to lift the charge of deicide from the Jews. But it also led to disappointments. In both 1967 and 1973, when Israel was engaged in life-and-death struggles for survival, the organized Protestant leadership, the Evangelicals excepted, was neither understanding nor friendly. And at this writing the Vatican has still not recognized the state of Israel.

We earlier called attention to the absence of a contemporary rabbi who commands national prominence and influence. We did not comment on the leadership of the federations where large, active donors are frequently advanced into top positions, usually for a limited term to assure that the honors can be broadly shared. As with the rabbinate, local distinction and local leadership do not translate easily into national prominence.

If we look to the presidents of the national Jewish organizations including the most prominent who have seats on the Conference of Presidents, which has been in existence since the mid-1950s and which became more active after the Six Day War, we cannot identify over this third of a century more than a handful of men who command a broad following among American Jews and among other Americans.

One explanation for the relative lack of distinction among these leaders is the way in which Jewish life is organized in the United States with its emphasis on localism, the split between the religious and the secular, the desire and need to share honors among many philanthropic volunteers, the avoidance of strong ideological positions, and the inherently volunteeristic nature of all institutions. These factors do not preclude the emergence of outstanding national leaders but they surely present formidable hurdles to their emergence.

Now that we have reviewed, if only in broad strokes, the principal institutional structures that provide the organizational framework for Jewish activities in the United States, one confronts a dilemma. It is easier to define and describe the structures than to analyze their dynamics. In the normal course of events one would expect group commitment to lead to organization-building and leadership, which in turn would result in the raising of revenues to meet communal goals.

I recall extended conversations with Reuven Shiloah in the mid-1950s, which centered around the likely erosion of support of American Jews for Israel as the older generation that had seen the emergence of the state and that had to absorb the immensity of the Holocaust would age and pass from the scene and a new generation would emerge that had not known Weizmann or Ben-Gurion. A third of a century later it is clear that Shiloah and I were unduly concerned; the flow of funds from American Jews has continued at an impressive level although they have been dwarfed by the assistance made available by the U.S. government.

The leadership issue took an unusual turn: American Jews borrowed most of their leadership from Israel. Over the years it was Golda Meir,

Moshe Dayan, Abba Eban, Yigdal Allon, Shimon Peres, Menachem Begin, Yitzchak Shamir, and a large number of senior generals who made periodic visits to the United States to address overflow audiences and who spent considerable time talking with American visitors in Israel. Moreover, the successive ambassadors from Israel to the United States and their senior staff members spent much if not most of their time providing the critical ingredient of leadership and information to the never-ending fund-raising affairs.

One can conclude that the state of Israel through its senior representatives provided American Jewry with the leadership it had not provided for itself that infused life and spirit into its basic federation infrastructure. In turn, of the trilogy — commitment, organization, fund-raising — the availability of the Israeli leaders made it possible to reverse the process: expanding fund-raising activities strengthened the extant organizations, which in turn provided a broader and stronger basis for commitment.

7

Jews and Other Minorities

Among the principal reasons for the 1920–24 federal legislation that severely restricted immigration into the United States was the growing opposition among various native-born groups to the large-scale inflow of Jews from Eastern Europe. This does not imply that if there had been fewer Jewish immigrants to the United States in the pre-World War I era, the restrictive legislation would not have been enacted. Yet latent and overt anti-Semitism made a significant contribution to the passage of the new immigration act. The nativists, eugenicists, trade unionists, anti-Wall Streeters, and many more groups believed that more harm than good would result to the American people from the large annual additions of Jews and other East Europeans, who had been landing mostly on the East Coast ever since the early 1880s. While the leaders of the Jewish community had helped to persuade several earlier presidents to veto restrictive legislation, the combination of forces unleashed by wartime patriotism, anti-Red scares, and the recession of 1920–21 were too powerful for them to overcome. The new restrictions were passed by large congressional majorities and signed into law by Presidents Warren Harding and Calvin Coolidge.

Despite the immigration of over 2 million Jews in the short period of one-third of a century, from the early 1880s to the outbreak of World War I, the vast majority settled in New York City and other major cities on the East Coast, in Chicago, and in a few of the larger cities of the Middle West such as Cleveland, Milwaukee, and St. Louis.

Although the Jewish leadership had made an effort to have some of the heavy traffic from Europe deflected to Galveston, Texas, with an eye to facilitating the settlement of Jews in the Southwest and the West, it had had only limited success. It is estimated that no more than 10,000 Jews used this alternative port of entry.

The choice of New York City and other East Coast cities as preferred places of settlement; the relatively limited relocation after the immigrants took up initial residence; the failure of the alternative debarkation port in Texas; the large expanse of the United States — all meant that a great many Americans, even at the height of the Jewish immigration, never had had any direct knowledge of or personal interaction with a Jew.

Let me give two illustrations. When I was a student at Heidelberg, I became friendly with a young couple, natives of Wisconsin, who had attended and graduated from the university in Madison. The husband told me that he had never met a Jew until he enrolled in the university and he was still perplexed by a Jewish custom that he had encountered. He had been invited to a Jewish wedding and they served ice cream before the main meal. He wanted to know whether this was a universal Jewish custom or not. Perplexed, I finally solved the riddle: according to the dietary laws, a dairy dish had to precede the meat course!

Only the other day, a considerably younger Columbia colleague, about sixty, told me that his bride and he went to a lodge on Keeser Lake in Maine for their honeymoon in the early 1950s. They were the first Jewish guests who had ever stopped there and during the course of their fortnight's stay many of the other guests sought them out. These guests had never before had any personal contact with Jews. It may not be entirely beside the point to ask how many of the active members of the Ku Klux Klan with its avowedly anti-Semitic platform have had any personal acquaintance with Jews. The same question can be raised about the members currently enrolled in the neo-Nazi movement centered in the Northwest.

But that is no reason for surprise. It is the concept of the Jew as the devil incarnate — a person with horns — who is the enemy that must be attacked and destroyed. The lack of personal knowledge of Jews removes all restraints and inhibitions from the extreme anti-Semite.

Social scientists and other observers of the American experience have sought for an explanation of the differentially rapid educational and occupational advance of the East European Jewish immigrants. We will leave in abeyance for now whether in fact the data confirm that the advance of Jews was so much more rapid than that of other groups such as the Irish, the Italians, and the Slavs.

One datum must be accepted: a high proportion of all Jewish immigrants started at the very bottom of the ladder as street peddlers, as factory or home workers, as laborers. As Jacob Riis and others who studied New York's lower East Side at the turn of the century have made clear, life in the tenements could not have been more brutish. The slums were characterized by overcrowding, unhygienic conditions, marginal

income, crime, prostitution, generational conflict, and many other environmental negatives. But within a single generation, and often before,
many families had escaped. And within two generations, the East Side
origins of most of the Russian Jewish immigrants were lost to all except
the historians.

In the early post-World War II decade when Louis Finkelstein was
planning to edit his ambitious project on *The Jews*, which was later
published in two volumes, he asked me to prepare the chapter on the
economic history of the Jews in the United States. If I were unable to take
on the assignment, he asked me to suggest alternative authors. I responded immediately that I was not qualified to write the definitive
article that he wanted and needed, and I suggested that he get in touch
with Simon Kuznets, who later became a Nobel Laureate in economics
and, in the view of many of us, was the outstanding twentieth-century
scholar on the transformation of modern economies. Fortunately, Finkelstein persuaded Kuznets to accept the assignment and we therefore have
an insightful, carefully crafted chapter that analyzes the economic experience of Jewish immigrants in the United States against the background of
their roles and experiences in Russia and Poland. Kuznets, himself an
immigrant, was uniquely qualified to see the development of Jews in the
United States against the backdrop of their earlier experiences on the
fringes of modern Russian capitalistic development.

Kuznets called attention to the following important facts: many Jews
who came to this country had taken several important steps while still in
Europe to transform themselves into an industrialized people: they had
an above-average level of literacy, they were highly urbanized, many of
them had acquired industrial skills in textiles and related fields, another
significant group was engaged in wholesale or retail trade, and, very
important, the number of children per family was several notches below
that of the non-Jewish population. Using these characteristics and behavior patterns, Kuznets was able to chart the educational, occupational,
and income changes that characterized the several generations of immigrants in the United States.

While borrowing heavily from Kuznets, I tried my hand at an interpretation of the characteristics of the American economy during the 1920s–
80s that facilitated the advance in the well-being of such a large segment
of American Jews, advances that appear to have been more rapid than for
other ethnic or racial groups. The American Jewish Committee sponsored a series of lectures and later published a book, *Jewish Life in
America*, edited by Gladys Rosen, in connection with the nation's Bicen-
tennial celebration. My chapter was entitled "Jews in the American Economy: The Dynamics of Opportunity."

I singled out five factors that were critically important for the above-average mobility of the Jews. The first was the fact that Jews were in the right place at the right time. They took up residence and found work in the nation's largest metropolises at the time when these centers were entering the period of their most rapid growth.

The second favorable factor relates to education, more correctly, educational opportunities. Hard as it is to believe in the year 1988, schools in metropolitan centers earlier in the century were several steps in advance of schools in other communities; and schools in the Northeast were ahead of those in most other regions. Further, New York City, which at that time was home to about half of all American Jews, financed out of local taxes high-quality public colleges – City College, Hunter, and later Brooklyn and Queens – thereby providing important help to the children of low- and modest-income families who sought to prepare themselves for a wide array of professional and civil service positions including accounting, law, medicine, teaching, social work, journalism, and other occupations open to college graduates or to those who went on to pursue graduate or professional training.

As a student in the New York City public schools prior to my admission to Columbia College in 1927, I can attest firsthand to the fact that the public schools had neither exciting staff nor interesting curricula, but that they did set reasonable performance standards. High school graduates were prepared for college; those who dropped out in their tenth or eleventh year were functionally literate and were employable across the wide band of New York's expanding service sector.

The question is often raised whether or not Jews were propelled toward higher education and the professions because of their strong cultural tradition and whether or not this tradition gave them an advantage in pursuing their educational goals because they had greater facility with ideas, words, and numbers. I have no doubt that some Jews are bright, that others are precocious, and that many are strongly motivated to succeed. What remains unclear, in fact equivocal, is whether they have on average a superior intellectual endowment, or not.

On balance, I believe the higher intellectual achievement of many Jews is a result of environmental factors, including extended family responsibility to not only the needy but the able; smaller family size, which made more dollars available per child; greater openness to educating girls as well as boys; the preference of Jews to prepare for entrepreneurship and/or independent professions where they will be less dependent on the good will and support of non-Jews; and the powerful "demonstration effect" of the success of the German Jews, which underscored the opportunities that were available to the new immigrants if they worked hard and obtained a few breaks.

The third potent factor contributing to the advance of second- and third-generation Russian Jews was the ongoing transformation of the metropolises where they were living from manufacturing to business and professional services. A considerable number of immigrants arrived in the United States with some prior experience as small-scale entrepreneurs, particularly in re-tailing. For hundreds of years many Jews had served as fiscal agents for the Polish nobility, as a consequence of which they developed considerable acu-men in money matters. Many young Jews learned about business—the buy-ing and selling of merchandise, real estate, stocks—by listening to the dinner conversations of their parents. Between these developmental exposures and the educational opportunities open to them, many were able to find jobs in the burgeoning service sector.

The fourth factor—the decline in religious prejudice across most of the American scene and particularly in business and the professions after World War II—proved to be a major boon to American Jews as it was to other minorities, particularly Catholics from eastern and southern Europe, that is, Slavs and Italians. Since the sectors that practiced discrimi-nation were declining in number and importance, Jews had broadened access to most if not all of the better-paying, prestigious positions in the American economy. For the first time a Jew could be elected or appointed the president of a large corporation, a major university, a foundation, or to a professorship at an elite institution; a Jew could advance into a top position in the local, state, or federal government. In fact, Jews had access to almost the entire range of desirable openings.

The preceding formulation does not imply, of course, that prejudice against Jews in the appointment and promotion process has evaporated. Rather, the emphasis is on the speed with which religious prejudice de-clined as a significant factor in personnel decisions. Most organizations no longer use a religious test in appointments and promotions, and the ceiling on Jews' aspirations to high positions has been effectively lifted.

The fifth contributory factor to improving the socioeconomic status of Jews has been the growth of the not-for-profit (government and nonprof-it) sector of the economy, which grew from under 15 percent in 1929 to over 30 percent in the ensuing half century. By residence and education, Jews were able to move into this expanding sector of the U.S. economy, which offered a substantial number of attractive positions, although the salaries they carried were somewhat below comparable earnings in the private sector.

If we consider the foregoing five factors from a temporal perspective, the following additional illumination can be extracted about the processes of mobility that had a benign effect on the Jews. Many offspring of East European parents had been born and educated in the United States when the post-World War I expansion of the economy took off. This meant that they were lifted by the rising tide of prosperity of the 1920s, particularly those whose fathers speculated successfully in real estate and securities. But the Great Depression wiped out many of the newly successful. In fact, Jews, like all other groups in American society, faced restricted opportunities and prospects during the elongated depression of the 1930s. One of my cousins, in his late twenties when the depression struck, never again found a regular job. His brother, a young physician, had to settle for an institutional appointment for several years before he could venture forth into private practice. And a second brother, seeking a position in the communications industry, found it necessary to Anglicize his name.

Many young Jews who graduated from college in the early 1930s faced such a bleak employment outlook that some of the most talented opted for high school teaching or became civil servants, positions that at least offered a living wage and security, although the work was routine and the opportunities for advancement were limited. The considerable flow of educated Jews and other upwardly mobile groups in the civil service in the 1930s helped to vitalize many bureaucracies. Their retirement in the 1960s and 1970s left serious gaps in many agencies. In the face of an acute shortage of jobs in the depressed 1930s, many college graduates decided that they had little to lose by continuing their studies. Many entered graduate school for advanced work in the natural or social sciences. As luck would have it, the big expansion in R&D as the United States began to mobilize for war created a greatly increased demand for mathematicians, physicists, chemists, engineers, and other scientists of such urgency that religious barriers were lowered or removed. As my friend Emanuel Piore, who later became chief scientist in the Office of Naval Research, recounts, when he started looking for a position in an industrial laboratory in the mid-1930s with a Ph.D. in physics from Wisconsin, he quickly learned that there was no point in his applying to either General Electric or Bell Laboratories. They simply did not hire Jews. But the war changed that quickly and permanently.

Another temporal event of major significance after the good days of the 1920s and the poor days of the 1930s was the long, sustained period of economic growth that started with the onset of mobilization and has continued, with minor interruptions, until the present (1988) — providing a supportive environment for educated persons to carve out successful careers for themselves over the past half century.

Because of location, family income, cultural values, and career goals, Jews account for the highest proportion of any group that enters and graduates from college or university. Currently over 90 percent of the college-age cohort of Jews attends college.

The women's "revolution" has also been a significant contributor to Jewish mobility by virtue of the earlier and greater participation of Jewish women in higher education, their lower fertility, and their urban location, which has made it easier for them to obtain jobs with career prospects.

One must look hard to find a dysfunctional trend. An assiduous search will reveal the relative underrepresentation of Jews living in the South and Southwest, which in the 1960s and 1970s enjoyed an above-average rate of economic expansion. But in the 1980s there has been a reversal in regional growth patterns. The East Coast cities have done quite well, all the way from Boston to Miami.

As of late 1988 there are many reasons to be concerned about the near-term and probably the long-term prospects of the U.S. economy, since there are so many distortions on both the domestic and the international fronts. An interruption of the elongated cycle of expansion that began in 1982 is almost certain; a serious interruption cannot be ruled out; a major international economic crisis is not impossible. Clearly, Jews like other Americans will be affected by the length and depth of whatever recession/depression occurs. But given their present geographic and occupational distribution, Jews should not be affected differentially. During the mid-1980s three important sectors of the U.S. economy have been seriously buffeted: agriculture, heavy manufacturing, and the oil-producing industry. While some Jews were victimized by these untoward developments, Jews as a group were less at risk than others.

Some observers believe that the success of Jews on the economic front in the United States has been so distinctive that it has been unique. But that appears to be an unwarranted conclusion. It is true that the mobility path of Jews was steeper than that of the Irish or the Italians, but it was not all that different, especially when allowance is made for such important factors as residential location and the stage of the nation's economic development. The more important contrast is between the progress of Jews and the recent efforts of blacks to advance up the occupational and income scales. Significant differences can be identified, even if some important parallels can be observed.

The start of Irish immigration into the Boston area began in the 1840s and 1850s, but it was not until the turn of the century that a significant minority had been able to attain middle-class status. And another generation or two had to pass before small numbers finally moved into higher levels of the economic and political structure. John F. Kennedy, who was the first member of the group to make it all the way to the White House, was a member of the sixth generation.

Other interesting aspects can be discerned by looking more closely at the acculturation of the Irish in the Boston area. The first is the depth and persistence of the hostility of the Protestant community and its entrenched leadership with which the Irish had to contend, not for a brief period but for successive generations. Even after demographic trends made it possible for the Irish to gain control of the local political system and to garner the important economic and occupational advantages that went with such control, the Boston establishment continued its exclusionary posture.

An amusing incident, which the principal party did not consider all that amusing, occurred in the late 1950s. John Gardner, then head of the Carnegie Corporation, asked me to attend a meeting between Dr. James Conant, former president of Harvard and former ambassador to West Germany, and a small group of black leaders who wanted to discuss the policy findings emerging from Conant's recent book on inner-city schools, which Carnegie had funded. Gardner thought that my presence and participation might help to take the edge off the confrontation. The discussion became ever more strained while I kept looking for an opening to ease the tension. At one point, Conant explained that his grandmother had a favorable attitude toward blacks and had supported the abolitionists. I broke in to suggest that the story indicated not that his grandmother had a positive view of blacks but only that she had a more negative view of the recently arrived Irish. Conant was not amused.

The Irish experience in Boston, paralleled by their experience in New York and other big cities where they also settled in large numbers, calls attention to the role that the Catholic church and parochial schools played in helping the newcomers make the transition, and the further boost that the newcomers derived from gaining control over the local political machine and the subsequent patronage. Americans date public welfare from the time of the New Deal in the mid-1930s, but in point of fact, the ward heelers of an earlier day used their political power and influence to assist many of their supporters who were in need of jobs or other favors.

In some respects the dominance of the Catholic church reduced the speed with which the Irish were able to move up the economic ladder. The church's opposition to birth control meant that Irish families tended to be large, with the result that there were fewer resources available for each of the children. Moreover, the church discouraged its members from sending their children to non-Catholic institutions of higher learning, which meant that the range and quality of the higher education to which they had access were restricted. Finally, the strong infrastructure that the church and its affiliated institutions were able to provide for its members encouraged them to look to each other rather than to the larger society in planning and structuring their lives. These supports in effect acted as barriers to the optimal acculturation and achievement of Catholic immigrants.

Unlike their Irish co-religionists, the Italians for the most part came much later, near the turn of the century. Their single largest concentration was in New York City, although sizable numbers settled in most of the larger East Coast and Middle West cities. Unlike the Irish, but similar to the Eastern European Jews, the Italian immigrants had to master a new language. Moreover, arriving a half century after the Irish, they found an industrial society moving into high gear. Hence their transition from the marginal agriculture that characterized the prevailing economy in southern Italy was more difficult than it had been for the Irish, who fled at the time of the potato famine when the United States was only beginning to industrialize.

The Italians, like the Irish, derived considerable support and succor from their church and parochial schools but, with the Irish well ensconced, the Italians were not able to develop the same close linkages to the political structure or to benefit as much from public-sector jobs.

But other factors were helpful to them. First, the large cities where they settled went from one construction boom to another and many Italians found employment in this sector with its opportunities for skill acquisition and relatively high wages. They brought from the old country the tradition of a strong patriarchal family structure, which helped to shape the behavior of young people who were caught in the cross-currents of a cultural transition.

Moreover, the Italians demonstrated skill in organizing activities that used an admixture of pecuniary talents, sophisticated organizational structures, and private power. This mix enabled them to accumulate capital and enabled the successful among them to provide jobs for other members of their community who needed a helping hand.

The Italian immigrants were conspicuous in one regard. Many came to this country because there were no opportunities at home. They could not make a living and start a family in their impoverished homeland. However, many expected to stay in the United States only long enough to make some money. They planned to return to Italy after they had accumulated sufficient funds to buy a tract of land where they could live among their own. No fewer than one out of every three Italians fell into this category of interim rather than permanent immigrants. Among the Jews, only a very small minority returned to Europe.

If we juxtapose the experience of the large Russian Jewish immigration to that of the Irish and the Italian, we can see one important difference not previously identified. The Russian Jews had the advantage of the "demonstration effect," which was a powerful spur to expanding their horizons. The success that their co-religionists, the German Jews, had achieved both raised their sights and encouraged them to invest all of their energies in improving themselves.

It is a matter of some interest to understand and explore the differential rates of socioeconomic progress achieved by these three groups of immigrants: the Irish, the Italians, and the East European Jews. It is equally important, however, to explore the experience of the blacks and to identify and assess the substantial differences between them and the European immigrants in their movements up the economic ladder, particularly the nature of the differences between blacks and East European Jews.

I find it incomprehensible that well-educated, well-informed members of the Jewish community argue that "since we made it, why can't the blacks?" Based on this premise, they oppose affirmative action, guidelines, quotas, and all the other paraphernalia of judicial and administrative interventions by government to speed the integration of blacks into the larger society and economy. The question of whether specific affirmative-action approaches should command continuing public approval and support fades in the presence of the antecedent question of whether the experiences of Jews and blacks are to be equated.

I had a cubicle in the Columbia library in the late 1930s only a few doors away from Gunnar Myrdal, who was writing his *An American Dilemma*. Regrettably, his conclusions are not part of the knowledge base of those who argue that the challenges facing blacks and Jews are substantially identical. Nothing could be further from the truth. Myrdal is the source for the following: as late as 1940, four out of every five blacks were still living in the South, the area of the country that President Roosevelt had identified as the nation's number one economic problem. The blacks in the South were primarily tenant farmers eking out a marginal living on ever more eroded land; much of the household's food arrived by the "toting" of black women who worked in white homes as domestics for a few dollars a week. The New Deal's public-sector employment and income-transfer programs made it possible for considerable numbers of southern blacks to escape from their highly confining and oppressive environment. The fortunate among them came North and got jobs on WPA or PWA.

Lynching was still an extra-legal method of controlling blacks, and

Tuskegee Institute kept and published the annual record of organized murders of blacks. The South, as noted above, was poor but as my friend Charles Johnson, the distinguished black sociologist and long-term president of Fisk University, used to remark, Mississippi (and by inference other southern states) educated whites off the backs of blacks. This oblique remark referred to the grievously uneven distribution of support for white and black schools. Small wonder that I found in 1953, when I was writing *The Uneducated*, that one out of every four black men of draft age in South Carolina had been rejected for military service during World War II because he was unable to pass the fifth-grade literacy test! And as late as 1956 I noted in the *The Negro Potential* that black men were still excluded from manufacturing jobs in the South except those in sawmills and the tending of blast furnaces.

Mention of *The Negro Potential* leads me to recall an unsettling episode in my research career. One night, close to midnight, I had a call from General Howard Snyder from southern Alabama, where President Eisenhower was vacationing, to the effect that the president, who had read my draft chapter on "The Negro Soldier," was very upset. He thought that I had the story all wrong, that I failed to deal properly with the facts, and that the whole tone was too apologetic. I told General Snyder to tell the president that I would pay close attention to his critique and that he would get a redraft shortly.

The term "apologetic" tipped me off. There is no question that on many objective indices the army data pointed to serious defects in the performance of many black soldiers. I presented the data but immediately offered extenuating interpretations. The analysis and the evaluation ran into each other. I rewrote the chapter and separated clearly and sharply fact from interpretation but added and subtracted nothing that had been in the first draft. I simply rearranged the argument.

The president read my new draft. When I next saw him at the White House, he said, "You know, Eli, there really isn't that much difference between all of us, blacks and whites. The chapter is okay."

Although the first blacks came to Virginia as early as 1619, it would be stretching the point only slightly to contend that the integration of blacks into the U.S. economy as free members in a competitive labor market dates not from 1619 but from 1941. I have suggested on occasion that the only sensible way of assessing the success of the blacks is to measure what has happened to them since World War II. Once again, Myrdal is my authority: except for very small numbers of professionals, businessmen, and civil servants, most blacks at the outbreak of World War II were either tenant farmers operating in the South at or below subsistence level or were employed in the North primarily on public programs.

Using 1941 as the baseline, we can see that two generations later a significant minority of blacks, circa one-third, have achieved middle-class status and income. This underscores the fact that more education and better jobs are contributing to the mobility of many blacks, just as they had earlier facilitated the advance of Jews and other minorities.

But if one-third of the blacks are on their way up, what about the other two-thirds who are trapped at or close to the lower end of the distribution, many of them requiring welfare payments for their support and the support of their dependents? Only an unimaginative analyst would argue that the sum total of affirmative actions is sufficiently weighty to overcome the continuing adverse effects of past and present racial prejudice and discrimination.

The difficulties that large numbers of blacks are experiencing in achieving a secure place for themselves in the increasingly sophisticated U.S. service economy is rooted in the following complex factors. First is the disruption that accompanies the large-scale migration of farmhands to an urban industrial and commercial environment. Since the outbreak of World War II, there has been a large-scale relocation of blacks from southern farms to southern cities and to the cities in the North and the West. Since housing segregation along racial lines is deeply embedded in most regions of the country and since whites relocate when their neighborhood begins to tip, most urban blacks are concentrated in ghettos in the inner cities. This concentration is reflected in poorly performing public schools, which find it next to impossible to surmount the cumulative disadvantages of a predominantly minority school population, many from single-parent families, characterized by low income and a host of neighborhood pathologies including crime and drugs. These overburdened schools, many led and staffed by persons who have given up on their pupils, fail to provide the new generation of black youngsters with the essential skills that they will need to become self-supporting.

The criteria identified earlier that helped to account for the significant progress of Jews and other minorities — time of arrival, location, community infrastructure, demonstration effects — are conspicuous by their absence in the case of the blacks. Over the long stretch, that is, from the end of the Civil War to the outbreak of World War II, blacks were in the wrong location; the South was so impoverished and had such a serious shortfall of total jobs that blacks were essentially excluded from all but the most menial work. When most blacks became urbanites, during and after World War II, they found an economy that increasingly hired workers on the basis of their educational qualifications. Unlike the experiences of other minorities of an earlier day, it was no longer possible for a young man or a young woman to get a job with prospects for advancement merely because he or she had native ability and wanted to work. The increasingly service-oriented economy requires recruits who have at a minimum a high school diploma. However, a third to a half of all blacks in the inner city complete their schooling without acquiring the requisite competences. Thus blacks were in the wrong place at the wrong time and, when they finally relocated, many faced an unbridgeable gap between their educational achievement and what employers desired and demanded.

Too little attention has been paid to the social isolation of blacks and the handicaps that such isolation imposes on people who are seeking to join the mainstream. I had never visited a black person's home until the president of Columbia University in the late 1950s asked me to represent him at a convocation at Maryland State College where he had accepted an invitation that he could not fulfill.

The night that I spent at President and Mrs. John Holland's home was my first such visit. The next time I met Dr. Holland was at a party at his home in Stockholm where he was serving as the U.S. ambassador to Sweden. I must add that the first black guest at our home is of even more recent date. We entertained in the early 1980s the members of the selection committee for the Revson Fellow Program at Columbia and their wives, which included one of my most distinguished black colleagues.

Although there were a few black students in each of my classes from the first grade through the completion of my doctorate and although I became quite friendly with some of them, there was little if any opportunity to visit back or forth. We lived on different blocks, in different neighborhoods, circulated among different groups. The preconditions for social intimacy were missing.

Southerners like to boast that the quality of social relations between whites and blacks has been much better in the racially sensitive South than in the more liberal North. But I was never able to see the basis for this sweeping generalization. In the late 1950s I was invited by the Southern Economic Association to talk on the racial aspects of manpower waste, a subject that, it was explained to me, no southerner could be asked to address. I accepted and was interested to discover that the meeting was held on the outskirts of Atlanta because none of the downtown hotels was willing to host a biracial group.

A few years later I was in Atlanta and had arranged ahead of time to meet with my former Columbia classmate, Dr. Brailsford Brazeal, the dean of Morehouse College. He was to pick me up in the lobby of my hotel, which he did but not without having to stare down a number of hostile people who indicated that he was intruding. When I joined him in the front seat of his car, he explained that we were both at some risk because whites were not supposed to ride in the front of a car driven by a black person. More revealing, Brazeal told me that each time that he drove out to the countryside to help blacks to register he never knew whether he would make it back to the city alive.

In 1963 when I was a visiting lecturer at Morris Brown College, one of the constituent institutions of Atlanta University, I was late in returning from a luncheon with Ralph McGill of the *Atlanta Constitution*. Some jokesters told my wife that I might never make it back, since white persons were often lost on the taxi ride from downtown to the college.

Atlanta, like many other large cities, has had a black mayor for a number of years; and the post-civil-rights period has seen a substantial improvement in the rules and customs governing social interactions between whites and blacks. But it would be a grievous mistake to underestimate the continuing difficulties that blacks face because of their substantial isolation from mainstream United States.

But there is more. We noted previously the important role of community infrastructure in helping Jews, Irish, and Italians get started and advance. The contemporary ghetto does not have a supportive infrastructure. The black churches cater in large measure to the middle class, many of whom return to their earlier neighborhoods to worship. Settlement houses or their modern equivalents are few and far between. In most cities with a large black population there are seldom entrenched, well-led local black political machines with sufficient power to insist on their share of the benefits from City Hall.

With time, some of the missing elements are being put in place. The number of black mayors in the nation's largest cities is a powerful reminder that the black community, like other outsider groups, is resorting to the ballot box to improve its ability to direct more benefits to its members. But as the confrontation of the late 1960s between the teachers' union and the local black communities in Brooklyn demonstrated, wresting power and jobs from entrenched groups is not easy. On the other hand, it should be noted that one of the principal avenues of economic progress for blacks, particularly in the expansive 1960s, was through enlarged opportunities in the public sector—local, state, and federal. Many of the new black middle-class owe their status to the civil service.

A word about the other potent criterion: the "demonstration effect," which we noted played a role in encouraging Russian Jewish immigrants to set and pursue ambitious goals. The conventional wisdom is that once a black family, especially one with school-age children, is in a position to escape from the ghetto, it will relocate to the suburbs to improve the social and particularly the educational opportunities available to its offspring. This means that many black youngsters growing up in the ghettos do not have firsthand exposure to black persons whose education has enabled them to design and achieve a better future for themselves. In a study that I conducted in Harlem with two black graduate students, we talked to black high school students who could not identify a single person in their acquaintanceship who had benefited from graduating from high school by securing a desirable, full-time job. (The study, entitled *Tell Me About Your School*, was published by the National Commission for Employment Policy, Washington, D.C., in 1979.)

To argue, as many have, that blacks should be able to match the record of educational and economic mobility achieved by Jews and other minorities without special assistance by government and the private sector ignores the importance of the criteria that we have identified as enhancing the mobility process.

The conventional wisdom among conservatives and neo-conservatives is to look to the weaknesses in the black family—unmarried pregnant teenagers, female-headed households, long dependency on welfare—as the prime causes for the continued economic backwardness of many blacks. Clearly, weaknesses in the black family are reflected in underperformance in school and later difficulties in the labor market.

In 1966 President Lyndon Johnson appointed a secret Task Force on the ghetto with George Shultz as chair and the remainder of the committee consisting of industrialists, black leaders, professionals, and a few academics, including myself. Several facets of the Task Force's experiences were noteworthy: it was well staffed; committee members made time to visit several ghettos and talk with the inhabitants; the agenda was wide open and with George Shultz's encouragement we were not inhibited, coming up with an action agenda that carried an annual price tag of between $13 and $18 billion. But our report never saw the light of day. All the copies were impounded by Joseph Califano of the White House staff acting on behalf of the president. The Vietnam War had first claim on all new dollars.

But my recalling the existence of this Task Force was for another purpose. One of the corporate executives began to play a broken record: whatever was wrong with the blacks resulted from the ever larger number of adolescent girls who were becoming mothers out of wedlock. In frustration I asked a fellow member, a distinguished lawyer who later went onto the federal bench, how long he thought it might be before the Supreme Court would rule that women had the right to determine whether they carried their fetuses to term or had an abortion. At a subsequent meeting he gave his answer: sometime in the early 1990s! Aside from his being far wide of the mark—the Supreme Court ruled as early as 1973—

my assumption that the availability of abortion would reverse the trend was also proved wrong.

But it is necessary to look at the causal chain of black poverty from the other end. Many young and older black men with limited education and with few if any skills are unable to get and hold jobs. Hence they are unable to support a wife and children. Unable to fit into the world of work, many drift over into the underground economy and to a life of crime and drugs. They develop a police record and serve prison sentences, which further militates against their ever getting regular jobs. A disturbingly large number become the victims of homicide.

It is easy to single out the weaknesses in the black family and to ascribe all of the ills facing the black community to that source. But there is a difference between easy and right. In the face of continuing oppressive racism, neighborhood decay, ineffective schools, and lack of employment opportunities for many black men, the weaknesses in the black family are as much the consequence as the cause of the continuing difficulties that such a large proportion of blacks face in a country to which they were first brought almost 400 years ago.

8

Israel

My first connection with Palestine was precipitated by the editor of *The Menorah Journal* asking me in the late 1930s to review A. H. Gordon's essays, which had recently been translated into English. It was not an easy book for a New Yorker with no firsthand knowledge of Palestine and with only limited knowledge of the East European immigrants who were Gordon's readers to assess. This Jewish Thoreau saw the cultivation of the land as the road to individual and national salvation. From my perspective, the redemption of the Holy Land by Jewish farmers might be a necessary but surely not a difficult condition for the reestablishment of a homeland that would provide a new life for its immigrants. The burden of my conclusion was that if Palestine were to become more than a burial ground for the pious, economic development policy would have to center on the growth of industry and commerce. Farming could never support more than a relatively few immigrants.

As noted earlier, the British, caught between their obligations as the Mandatory Power and rising Arab nationalism, sought to extricate themselves by raising the issue of the capacity of the country to absorb continuing large numbers of Jewish immigrants. On the basis of advice from prestigious commissions and under the strong promptings of its foreign and colonial officers, the British government decided to use the argument of absorptive capacity to justify placing severe limits on the flows of new immigrants in the late 1930s and thereafter. The book by Robert Nathan, Oscar Gass, and Daniel Creamer, *Palestine: Problem and Promise*, specifically addressed this issue and found the restrictive immigration policy based on absolute capacity to be specious, a conclusion accepted by the Anglo-American Commission of Inquiry.

A key aspect of Jewish experience in the Diaspora has been the capacity of successive Jewish communities to avoid being obliterated by catastrophes. While untold numbers of Jews suffered grievous losses, including life, limbs, and property, from the periodic outbreaks of government- or church-sponsored attacks on them, many Jews, faced with the alternative of apostasy or flight, opted to relocate in more favorable climes to start anew. The Grand Mufti of Jerusalem, living in exile after World War II, suggested that a statue to Adolf Hitler be erected in Tel Aviv, since Palestine would not have attracted the numbers of immigrant Jews required to establish the bridgehead from which the state eventually emerged without the persecution of the Jews by the Nazis.

My first visit to Israel was in the summer of 1953 following upon the Israeli government's request that the U.S. Department of State make me available to help develop a manpower policy and to advise on establishing a human-resources planning agency. During the next three and a half decades I have returned for a total of fifteen study-visits, all of which have been linked to issues of human resources and economic development.

During my first assignment I saw that the Israeli government faced a truly overwhelming number of urgent, even emergency problems, such as finding jobs and building permanent housing for the 100,000 or more immigrants from Muslim countries who were living in *Ma'arbarot*, temporary housing of barrackslike construction. My wife, who accompanied me, was so depressed by her first impressions that she would not leave the Ramat Aviv motel outside of Tel Aviv, which Teddy Kollek had selected for us as the most suitable accommodation in the coastal plain. Fortunately Milton Fried and his wife, Philoine, Sidney Hillman's daughter, came by on the weekend and took us to an attractive beach, which went far to counter the initial depressing impressions that had overwhelmed both of us. Fried was one of the few members of the U.S. embassy staff who was Jewish, and during the course of our summer's stay he was promoted from labor attaché to the Political Desk, an unusual move except to those who knew him. He was a person of high intelligence, superior analytic skills, and great sympathy and understanding. His early death deprived the labor movement — the Amalgamated Clothing Workers — (he had resigned from the State Department shortly after our visit) of one of its strongest staff members.

In the course of one weekend during that summer, the Israelis decided to relocate their seat of government from Tel Aviv to Jerusalem. They did so without prior consultation with the United States or the United Nations, each of which was strongly opposed to the move on juridical and political grounds. All of the U.S. embassy staff, regulars and consultants alike, were directed by the U.S. ambassador not to travel to Jerusalem to do business with Israeli officials but to insist that such meetings be held in Tel Aviv. As is so often the case with U.S. foreign policy, and more particularly with State Department rules and regulations, finding a balance between the short- and long-term interests of the United States is difficult. The U.S. embassy as well as the embassies of all the other large nations remain in Tel Aviv, but all of them conduct their basic work with the Israeli government in Jerusalem. As far as the long view is concerned, it is worth observing that successive U.S. presidents have used excellent judgment in the appointment and retention of American ambassadors to Israel. There are few ambassadorial positions of more complexity, diplomatic sensitivity, and potential domestic political fallout. On the basis of my continuing exposure to America's major embassies in Western Europe — in London, Paris, Bonn, and Rome — I would place the work of U.S. ambassadors to Israel over the years as equal or superior to their colleagues in Europe.

In 1953 the state of Israel was only five years old but the Jewish settlement of the country had its roots in the flow of immigrants that had begun toward the end of the nineteenth century, which meant that the building of the homeland had been under way for about sixty years. In addition to the miracle of statehood, much had been accomplished: Tel Aviv, Haifa, and Jerusalem boasted sizable populations, which on the surface and even beneath the surface were able to enjoy a Western style of life, although the average income was below, far below, that of the United States. The kibbutzim, especially those that dated back to the first and second *aliyah* (migration), had reached a respectable level of organization and productivity but the country was in the throes of a severe food shortage, since the surge in population resulting from the recent inflow of several hundred thousand new immigrants created a demand that even a highly responsive agriculture could not meet in the short term. Notwithstanding the food shortages, the more doctrinaire socialist collectives refused to alter their ideological bias, which prohibited them from hiring workers to supplement their labor supply. At the same time they generally resisted admitting to membership the recent immigrants from Muslim countries, although few of the immigrants would have opted had the opportunity been offered them. The gap between the oldtimers and the newcomers was immense. It involved religious principles and practices, political orientation, family structure, language, education, cultural background, skills, work attitudes — in fact every facet of individual, family, and community structures and lifestyles.

During the course of my two-month study-mission I met two U.S. experts whom the Treasury Department had sent over to help the Israelis control their incipient inflation and improve their intermediate and longer-range economic policy. Raymond Mikesell and Gordon Patterson asked me to explain to them the current Israeli policy to invest sizable capital sums in irrigation and farm equipment, in order to enlarge their agricultural output. The Mikesell-Patterson team could not understand the rationale for additional capital investment in agriculture, since the dollars would have to come from the United States and since there was such a large unemployed and underemployed labor pool. In their view, sensible economic policy would be for the Israelis to pursue a labor-intensive rather than a capital-intensive farm policy.

I acknowledged that they had a point but I believed that their perspective was too narrow. They simply had not taken into account the depth of the leadership's commitment to building a modern, egalitarian society. And a modern society had to look to the greater use of technology across the board — in agriculture, infrastructure, and industry. While I was able to challenge my U.S. colleagues' diagnoses and policy presumptions, I had no answer to the question of how Israel, with its limited natural resources, large numbers of poorly educated immigrants, limited land, high defense burden, embryonic industrial plant, and egalitarian goals, was going to move from where it was to where it wanted to go.

It was only at the very end of my stay that I found what I believed to be the key to the conundrum. There was little point in looking at the Israeli economy through conventional models of developed or developing nations. The only way to achieve perspective on developments in Israel was to look at the road it had traversed and then to make some projections based on its own development path. The justification for searching for such an idiosyncratic explanation seemed to be embedded in the following unique challenges that the young state faced: the differentially large inflow of immigrants, which was resulting in a substantial increase in its population and labor force; the critically important role of the Histadrut to which almost all wage and salaried employees belonged, which was often a silent and sometimes a noisy partner in governmental decision-making; the irreconcilable differences among the religious and secular sectors of the society, which included the former's wanting to establish a theocracy based on the Halachah. Ben-Gurion sought to keep the peace by agreeing from time to time to minor concessions to the religious parties, particularly in allowing them to control their schools.

In writing my report, I was in a quagmire. I had spent considerable time looking into problems of military manpower and had given three lectures to the General Staff on problems dealing with the selection and utilization of manpower. In my report, I recommended that the government should consider acceding to the pressures of the religious parties to make the call-up of young women voluntary rather than compulsory. In my view the utilization of women by the defense forces was neither particularly efficient nor effective and I saw little risk if a small number of ultra-Orthodox young women were, on the basis of conscience, exempted from military service.

Golda Meir, then secretary of labor, refused to accept my report and held up its publication for several months until, through the good services of Teddy Kollek, at the time director of the prime minister's office, I was advised to rewrite the recommendation to read that the government explore possible alternatives to compulsory service for women if, as, and when the security situation permitted.

A few additional observations may be added here of that first visit that provided me with the baseline against which I have continued to measure all later developments. Israel in 1953 was very much in a pioneering mode faced with the twin problems of building a state and absorbing hundreds of thousands of newcomers. Morale was high. The egalitarian principle dominated. The purchase of food was strictly rationed, except in hotels that catered to tourists from overseas. Doers rather than thinkers were at the helm. It was my first exposure to a Jewish community that downgraded the importance of education, learning, and scholarship. Ben-Gurion, who set the style, was the great pragmatist, keeping his eye on his principal goals of strengthening defense and increasing immigration while willing to compromise any and all of the never-ending stream of issues that came before his coalition government. On the basis of my continuing contacts with Ben-Gurion from 1946 until his death in 1973, I was impressed with the extent to which his policies were shaped by the following: a faith that in the event of a crisis, Diaspora Jewry would not let Israel down; a trust in the potential good will of the U.S. government even when he experienced, before and after Sinai, repeated evidence of noncooperation and hostility; a willingness to approve large-scale outlays without knowing where the money would come from; a conviction that the populace and the leadership were in broad agreement about what needed to be done and that no matter how difficult the challenges might be, the national elan would not falter.

Another insight into Ben-Gurion's down-to-earth approach to people and issues. On one of my early visits he engaged me in conversation about Dwight Eisenhower and Adlai Stevenson. Unlike most U.S. Jews, who were enthusiastic Stevenson supporters, Ben-Gurion told me of a long conversation that he had had when Stevenson visited Jerusalem and his conclusion that Stevenson would not perform well in a crisis. According to Ben-Gurion, Stevenson saw too many angles and could not cut through to the heart of the issue. Although Ben-Gurion had had many reasons to be uneasy about the Eisenhower-Dulles team, which on balance had not been particularly friendly or supportive, he concluded that Israel would be better off if Ike were reelected.

Although Ben-Gurion was somewhat cavalier about money, that was less true of Eliezer Kaplan, the key guardian of the purse while the state was in the process of formation, and of his younger associate and successor, Levi Eschkol. But all of the leadership shared one view, especially when dealing with American Jews: give us the tools (money) and we'll do the job. I had tried to persuade Kaplan when he had talked to our Washington group at war's end that the Yishuv could attract a number of able young American Jews who were finishing their tours of duty in the military or in civilian defense assignments to work in Palestine for a year or two. This would add a significant increment to the skill pool. It was my belief that some who would sign up for a short-term tour of duty might eventually decide to stay. With a long list of unsolved and perhaps insoluble problems, including the successful resettlement of the former inmates of DP camps, the search for arms and dollars to build up the Jewish community's defense capabilities, and the need to finance a great many other priority undertakings, Kaplan understandably gave my human-resources suggestion short shrift.

Kaplan's response did not surprise me. What did is that none of his colleagues and successors ever evinced any real interest in tapping the sizable pool of U.S. talent across a wide array of fields — business, government, science.

I can understand and sympathize with the Israeli leadership, which, after so many years of difficulties, opposition from the Mandatory Power, lack of responsiveness from the civilized world during the Holocaust, wanted to work out its own solutions to its own problems. Why else a state? But as a specialist in human resources, acutely aware of the handicaps that the new state labored under in coping with large immigration, heavy defense expenditures, and isolated from the regional market, I found it foolish to the point of irresponsibility for the Israelis to limit their requests to Diaspora Jewry for dollars and pounds and not to include high in its priorities the borrowing of business and technical skills that could speed the growth of a viable industrialized economy. But that was not to be. In fact, the borrowing has been in the opposite direction. A considerable number of Israelis have moved to the United States where a few have contributed significantly to building up conventional and high-tech businesses and making contributions in other areas.

The Israeli leadership was slow to recognize the barriers to successful *aliyah* for young Americans and the need to explore alternative approaches. Years passed before the Jewish Agency and the government of Israel realized that they had much to gain from establishing summer camps for Jewish youth, although the Hebrew University moved early to expand its offerings so as to attract numbers of young Americans willing to spend a year abroad.

In times of crises, such as after the Yom Kippur War, Israel has been able to attract volunteers willing to come for six months or a year to help on any task that needed doing. And over the decades smaller numbers of young visitor-workers have come from Europe, including numbers of non-Jews, to work on the kibbutzim.

But the most skillfully organized efforts to attract young people came in more recent times when various sectors of the Orthodox community in the United States decided to send many of their young people to Israel for an extended period of full-time study directed exclusively to deepening their knowledge of the sacred texts. Many new yeshivas have been built in the last two decades, a considerable number in the Old City.

In assessing the growing stridency of the ultra-religious groups on the Israeli scene, one must note the considerable flow of dollars from their U.S. supporters and the reinforcement that the steady stream of dedicated students from the United States contributes by way of manpower, enthusiasm, and commitment.

On my second trip to Israel in the spring of 1956, I became more aware about two other aspects of Israel's human-resources problems. The first concerned the relatively small proportion of the age group who made it through secondary school. And the related phenomenon was the gross differences in educational achievement especially at college and university level between the Ashkenazi and the Sephardic communities.

The kibbutzim operated schools through the eighth or ninth grade and generally resisted sending their young people away to continue their education. They were afraid that the young people might not return and the collective would lose membership.

A look at the data revealed, however, that the dropout rate in urban schools was likewise high, particularly among lower-income groups who found the tuition payments onerous and who saw little point to prolonging the educational experience of their children. But money and parental attitudes aside, many of the children of recent immigrants disliked their schools. Only a few in the higher grades were able to meet the standards.

My studies in the United States on *The Uneducated* (1953) had revealed wide differentials in educational achievement among subgroups based on race, location, and income. I therefore made a special plea to Goria Josephtal, then minister of labor, to find some money to provide scholarships for able youngsters from the Sephardic community. I warned that unless the establishment moved early to nurture a leadership cadre from among the recent immigrants, the country would eventually face a serious split between the older and the newer settlers. The growing tensions in recent years between the haves and the have-nots largely reflects the timing of family immigration and the educational achievement of their children. Lack of attention and lack of resources to narrow the gap in years past will continue to extract a heavy toll in the years ahead. I recall an early conversation with Ben-Gurion (probably in the early 1960s) in which I challenged him about the failure of the Sephardim to rise in the military. His reply astonished me: he told me that one of his secretaries was a Sephardi. It should be noted, however, that in 1986 the chief of staff of the army was of Oriental background as is the current secretary-general of the Histadrut.

The response of the Israelis to the inadequacy of their educational system was slow in coming but it came. On one of my later visits, I called on Abba Eban, who was at the time the minister of education. He enlisted my help to discuss the opening chapter that Ben-Gurion had drafted to serve as the introduction to the government's *Yearbook*. Ben-Gurion had written that everybody who wanted to go to the university should be able to do so. Because of budgetary restraints, Abba Eban was facing great difficulties in improving elementary and secondary education. I cautiously raised the subject later with Ben-Gurion, not head-on, because he never reacted well to criticism, especially from outsiders who were inadequately informed about issues on which he had long reflected. Ben-Gurion told me how he had taught himself Greek and the pleasures he derived from his annual retreats when he was able to study the Bible and read the Greek classics. He saw no reason why any farmer or construction worker or for that matter any unskilled laborer who wanted a higher education should not be entitled to go to the university. Eban was right to be upset about priority investments, but Ben-Gurion would not change his introduction.

In the early years the higher educational structure in Israel consisted of the Hebrew University in Jerusalem, the Haifa Technion (engineering), and the Weizmann Institute (Rehovot, south of Tel Aviv). Despite the weaknesses in the basic school system, the institutions of higher learning expanded: Tel Aviv University; Bar Ilan University (also in Tel Aviv — the only institution under religious auspices); Haifa University; and Ben-Gurion University in Beersheba, established to serve the southern area.

In one of my reports I urged caution and restraint in establishing new medical schools on the ground that Israel was attracting from overseas a considerable number of physicians; that some Israelis were being sent by their families to study medicine abroad; and that the last thing that the country needed was a surplus of physicians. My recommendations notwithstanding, Tel Aviv University started a conventional medical school, which has been admitting forty U.S. students a year subsidized by New York state; and the medical school at Beersheba, established by Moshe Prywes, the former director of Hadassah Medical Center, has focused on the education of primary-care physicians, many of whom, it was hoped, would decide to remain and practice in the southern area.

The original big three — Hebrew University, the Technion, and Weizmann Institute — as well as the newcomers have nurtured groups of "friends" in the United States and other parts of the Diaspora to assist in raising capital and maintenance funds, but with the passage of time more and more of their total budgets have become a government responsibility.

As far as the health-care sector is concerned, the Israeli scene is increasingly ineffective from the viewpoint of organization and financing, as well as from the vantage of physician and patient satisfaction. Since the Histadrut was in existence for many decades before the establishment of the state, it had put in place many services that in other countries would have fallen under the aegis of the government, services that it continued to provide after the state came into existence. The health-care system continues to be dominated by the Kupat Holim, a subsidiary of the Histadrut. The government, however, controls and operates many of the large hospitals except the lead institution — Hadassah Medical Center in Jerusalem. Israel devotes about 7.5 percent of its gross national product (GNP) to health care, but it is likely that this figure is an understatement because of the underreporting of fees by private practitioners. Israelis use ambulatory-care services heavily, ten visits per capita per annum compared to four in the U.S., most of which are provided by clinics of the Kupat Holim. Except for a few senior clinicians at the major medical centers, physicians are disgruntled by the conditions under which they are forced to practice and the small salaries that they are paid. A few years ago they engaged in a long strike.

In December 1986 I gave the fourth Moshe Prywes Lecture at Ben-Gurion University at Beersheba, in which I sought to assess the Israeli health-care system and to forecast its future. The title of my address was "The Coming Crisis in the Israeli Medical Care System." The roots of the crisis follow: one cannot operate an egalitarian health-care system in a country with a nonegalitarian distribution of income, which characterizes Israel today; the hospital system is badly in need of rationalization and remains unduly centralized and bureaucratized; the heart of the emerging crisis stems from the shortfall in financing. Israelis want a level of medical services far in excess of the funds currently available to provide it. Finally the disgruntlement of physicians is a source of growing vulnerability (see *Israel Journal of Medical Services* 23, no. 3, 1987).

The principal goal of my successive study-missions to Israel in the

1960s and 1970s was to explore the extent to which the evolving quality of the labor force was facilitating or retarding the ability of the economy to grow, to increase its productivity, and to expand its exports — all essential steps in the evolution of Israel toward economic independence. Pinchus Sapir was the minister of finance in successive governments and he was responsible for overseeing the development of the Israeli economy. He was a man of great energy, drive, commitment and, above all, self-confidence. He had little respect for academicians and even less for experts, domestic or foreign. I liked him and I think he liked me because I never came to him with simple solutions as did Abba Lerner and Milton Friedman or some of the economists at the Hebrew University who believed that one or another of their favorite nostrums would put most things right.

Sapir basically was a deal-maker offering concessions, subsidies, tax benefits to entrepreneurs who were willing and able to start new enterprises — or expand existing ones — especially if they could provide jobs for the new immigrants. He knew, just as well as his critics, that the expansion of the textile industry was not likely to prove profitable over the long run. But Sapir lived in the short run and he needed more jobs *now*, even more than he needed better jobs a decade hence.

The Palestine Economic Corporation (PEC) in the United States, a Brandeis creation, was still chaired by my father-in-law, Robert Szold, during my first visits to Israel. He and some — but by no means all — of his board members were restive about the "interferences" of the Israeli government in the market place. They looked askance at Eschkol's and Sapir's deal-making. I tried to explain to the PEC Board that it was no use to rail against the Levantizing of the Israeli economy. The Israeli government was and would continue to be a major player in the economy, and deal-making by ministers was inevitable.

Certainly the American critics had ground for concern. If the Israeli economy depended more on deals with government officials than on market tests of productivity and profits, the outlook for establishing a self-sufficient economy was bleak. But there were good and sufficient reasons for continuing government involvement. It was important to speed the absorption of the newcomers, and the existence and persistence of high levels of unemployment would have slowed further *aliyah* from the United States and other Western countries and would also have increased the emigration of Israelis.

The centrality of the government in the development of the Israeli economy derived in no small measure from the prominent role that it played in obtaining funds from abroad: reparations from Germany, aid and loans from the United States government, contributions from Diaspora Jewry via annual appeals and later through the sale of Israeli bonds, and finally through private-sector borrowings. Nahum Goldmann, long-time Zionist but better described as a citizen of the world, played the leading role in convincing Konrad Adenauer to take the lead in persuading Germany to pay reparations both to individual Jewish victims of German expropriation and to the Jewish people represented by the state of Israel. With the support of Ben-Gurion, and with technical assistance from Dolleck Horowitz, the president of the Bank of Israel, Goldmann pulled off this coup that funneled many hundreds of millions of dollars into the state of Israel.

The staff of the Israeli embassy in Washington played an important role in the early 1950s by providing informal advice and assistance to the U.S. Congress as it began in a small way to provide money and technical assistance to a number of developing countries, including Israel. The Israeli embassy staff also worked hard to interest the Pentagon in easing the young state's needs for weaponry via loans, grants, and the transfer of surplus equipment. Interest on the part of the White House and/or key congressional leaders in those early days was important in moving the Pentagon from its neutral and sometimes negative position based on its disinclination to do anything that would upset the Arabs.

The Yom Kippur War in 1973 found the vulnerable Israeli forces dependent to an extraordinary degree on the emergency shipment of U.S. tanks and other equipment to replace its heavy losses during the first days of the battle. At this writing total U.S. government support for Israel amounts to approximately $3.5 billion, the highest level of U.S. aid given to any country.

With the advantages of hindsight, one can today recognize many questionable practices that became ingrained in the Israeli government's use of foreign funds flowing into the country from German reparations, U.S. government aid, and contributions from Diaspora Jewry, primarily from the United States. It would have taken a miracle, possibly several miracles, for Israeli officials to refrain from using some part of these monies to raise the living standards of the population and to "buy off" some of the political opposition. The large capital inflows also made it easier for Sapir to broaden and deepen his deal-making strategy of economic development.

The relative casualness about money is reflected in the following story. On one of my trips in the 1960s I called on Ben-Gurion to learn firsthand about his current preoccupations. He told me that he had as recently as the preceding week made me famous by stating in a debate in the Knesset that a distinguished American economist had told him in London (where we had met the year before) that "economics was not a science." I agreed that was the burden of what I had said, but I went on to add, "That doesn't mean that money doesn't count."

The dynamics of Israel's economic development was fueled by large capital inflows under the control of the officialdom who were directly responsible for the investments in defense, the Dead Sea, housing, irrigation, utilities, and other leading sectors. For many years the senior economic minister (Sapir) was in the strategic position of "doing favors" for public enterprises and various collective bodies, most of which were politically allied with the Labor party of which he was a key leader.

It is difficult even in retrospect to see how a much different development path could have been charted and followed. The entrepreneurial group was small; the Histadrut was a reality; the fledgling state required a steady inflow of funds to finance infrastructure investments; there were important political advantages to "buying off" some of the small parties that the reigning coalition needed to assure its continuance in office. What we do know from the vantage of a lengthened perspective is that such concentrated political control over such large sums meant that sooner or later a reckless leadership, without adequate self-discipline or experience, could pull the entire structure down, which almost happened during the runaway inflation in the second administration of Menachem Begin in the early 1980s.

Since there was little monitoring over the decades by any of the principal funders—the German government, the U.S. government, and the United Jewish Appeal—it is surprising that the Israelis did not get into serious trouble before the 1980s. There were occasional trial balloons from concerned supporters in the United States to the effect that one or another Israeli-American advisory/consultative group should be established to inform both the Israeli government and the American Jewish community about funding requirements and allocations. But the Israeli leadership was understandably reluctant to complicate further its decision-making processes by requesting advice from outsiders who in the last analysis had no political authority or responsibility. And if truth be told, most of the American Jewish leadership did not press to share in the decision-making process. For many years they had accepted the idea that they would raise money for Israel; the spending decisions would be made by the Israelis.

The first and perhaps the only instance of significant "foreign" leverage on the Israeli government in developing new financial and economic policies has been exercised by the U.S. Department of State, specifically through Secretary Shultz's ongoing consultations with several prominent Jewish economists in the United States whom the Israelis accepted as consultants because they were both competent and friendly. Since the

U.S. government has been making grants and loans to Israel of $3.5 billion annually, the Israelis were in no position to ignore such constructive advice.

In the early 1970s the Israeli leadership began to realize that the future of its economy was likely to be increasingly dependent on high-tech developments. While progress has been slower than initially anticipated, it has been sufficient to strengthen the conviction that this is the preferred road for Israel to pursue. In the mid-1960s I was asked by the Israelis to take a close look at their scientific and professional human resources. As a result of this inquiry I became impressed with the potential for R&D-based industry. But at that time, there was little if any follow-up to my report. The take-off in R&D took place in the 1970s and the subsequent progress has been impressive. In 1985 and again in 1986 I visited in Jerusalem an engineering design center, which a large U.S. computer manufacturer had recently established to take advantage of the engineering talent in the country. The training engineer from the United States told me that, based on his personal experience, he thought that the young Israeli staff showed more promise than the comparable Japanese staff with whom he had recently worked in Tokyo.

I took pride and pleasure in the fact that my father-in-law through his own gifts supplemented by gifts of his friends established the Robert Szold Institute for Applied Research at the Hebrew University, an undertaking that I believe my enthusiasm for the development of high-tech industry in Israel helped to encourage. In mid-1988 a report of actions of the Scientific Committee of the Institute pointed to the following recent subventions: drug efficiency studies using a bio-erodible novel formulation of indomethacin; development and characterization of electro-optimal switches; polyneurophin transformations in new hydrogenated canola oil; fermentation of mushrooms for flavor preservation. There are many opportunities for slippage between the laboratory and the market, but if only one in five or one in ten research projects proves successful, the investments will be more than justified. Moreover, Israel has no better resource to exploit than its brainpower.

The second critical development for the long-term restructuring of the Israeli economy occurred as a result of the state of Israel's new relationships with the European Economic Community, which were initially established in 1975 and which have become closer with the passing years. The import protection provided local manufacturing had to be dismantled and Israeli exporters must now compete without export subsidies in the European markets, which have become increasingly open to them. After a third of a century of protection and subsidies, Israeli manufacturers at home are increasingly exposed to foreign competitors, a salutary discipline for those who have the potential to make the grade.

A third important structural change with long-term consequences for the Israeli economy was put in place in 1985 when the United States and Israel signed an agreement setting up the Free Trade Area, which has resulted in a substantial increase in trade between the two countries.

Important as the United States and American Jews have been in providing political and economic support for the state of Israel during its formative years, the key to the growth and survival of the new state must be sought in its internal development. There are many Israelis, as well as many friends of Israel in the Diaspora, who have been deeply unsettled by several recent trends, particularly by the growing internal support for the permanent annexation of the West Bank, the ethnic and class conflicts between the older and the newer immigrants, and the no-compromise attitudes and behavior of the ultra-Orthodox. A few observations about each follow.

In my report on the Israeli government in the fall of 1967, some few months after the Six Day War, I assessed the human-resources implications of the vast new Arab population that had come under the control of the Israelis. I realized that the subject might be considered out-of-bounds even for a friendly consultant, so I decided to take informal soundings with several senior members of the cabinet. On demographic grounds alone, I was inclined to recommend the early disgorging of the newly added Arab population. Each of the ministers assured me that such a recommendation would be well received and I was free to make it. The Israeli government published my report, which contained a strong recommendation for the early give-back of people and land — since the two went together. With the passage of every year, now more than two decades ago, old assumptions and proposed solutions receded into the background and new realities and ambitions came to the fore. The only reason not to be totally despondent about the long delay in reaching a satisfactory settlement about the annexed Arabs is the demographic imperative: Israel cannot remain Israel and absorb a million additional Arabs. Only a small group of extremists believes that most or all of the West Bank Arabs can be relocated to the East Bank. Consequently, a negotiated settlement must remain on the agenda.

There is little to be gained in reassessing at this point in time whether the Labor party treated the Jews from Muslim countries unfairly and therefore set the stage for Begin's first and second victories in 1977 and in 1981. What is clear in retrospect is that the majority of Orientals felt that they had been shabbily treated (or ignored) and when the opportunity offered they went with those who promised to help them. From my perspective, among the few lasting contributions of the Begin years were the gains in the political power of the Sephardim, a necessary step in the evolution of Israeli society in which they are now the majority.

The cultural gap between former professors from Germany and immigrants from the Atlas Mountains must be calculated in centuries, possibly in millennia. No observer should have expected anything less then tensions, conflicts, and hostility between the old settlers and the new. There is no definitive evidence as to whether intergroup conflicts are beginning to recede or whether they are still accelerating. But my judgment is that the level of conflict has probably crested and that powerful long-term forces are at work that with time will narrow the gap between the two groups. The number of marriages between the two groups is increasing; family size of the younger generation of Sephardim and the Sabras has practically been equalized; the educational and occupational achievements of the newcomers continue to improve, though they lag considerably behind the oldtimers. The fact that many Orientals have a deep distrust, often a hatred, of Arabs at whose hands they suffered for so long makes peaceful negotiations with Jordan and Syria more difficult; but they also have a deeper understanding of Islam and how it affects the lives of the Arabs.

There are good reasons that many Israelis and many friends of Israel are disturbed and distressed by the rising stridency of the ultra-Orthodox and their tactics to intimidate and otherwise force the moderate majority into conformance with the Halachic code. These intimidation tactics have been reasonably successful to date only because of the long-delayed reform in the Israeli electoral machinery, which still makes it possible for the small religious parties to win a few seats in the Knesset that provide them with the bargaining chips they need to force their preferences onto the majority.

Disturbing as this trend has been, and remains, it should not be exaggerated. The non-Orthodox remain in the vast majority and it is highly unlikely that this will change. It is also unlikely that the non-Orthodox will tolerate more and more restrictions on their own behavior. The Conservative and Reform Jews in the United States and elsewhere in the Diaspora have been able to shore up successive governments from buckling under to the extremists' demands. And one must allow for the long-term moderating influence of the Sephardim, most of whom eschew religious extremism.

It would be amusing if it were not so fraught with danger to domestic peace and tranquillity to note that in 1987 the votes of eight Arabs aligned with the Labor party blocked the Knesset from defining "who is a Jew" according to strict Halachic criteria. The vote was disturbingly close despite the strong opposition voiced by the Reform and Conservative leadership in the United States.

The threat from the ultra-Orthodox may worsen before it lessens, but it would appear from the foregoing that difficult and distasteful as their tactics have been and continue to be, the future will not be theirs.

On my first visit to Israel, in 1953, Teddy Kollek arranged for me to visit with Moshe Dayan, then on leave from the army and pursuing studies at the Hebrew University. At the end of a fascinating and far-ranging conversation on a Sabbath morning, Dayan asked me to step out on his balcony, which had a fine view of Tel Aviv. He pointed out the areas where the city had recently expanded and then went on to share his prevision of things to come. He told me that he foresaw a much greater expansion of the city to the south and the east, with the probable doubling and doubling again of the population, at which point Tel Aviv would become as unattractive as most rapidly expanding urban concentrations. He said he could see the hundreds of thousands of new urbanites many of them with no feeling for or interest in the city except as a place to live and work. And he was certain that it would be only a few years before the clean atmosphere would be replaced by smog, the inevitable by-product of urban experience. He was a prophet who saw deeply into the future and didn't like what he saw.

The special quality of the Israeli experience was impressed upon me some years after that event. I had driven down with Teddy Kollek and Isaiah Berlin from Jerusalem to have lunch with Ben-Gurion, who was living at Sdeh Boker, making a short stop at Beersheba, at the time a small, sleepy desert town. At luncheon we were nine in total, the other guests being Walter Eytan, at the time Israel's ambassador to France, Isaac and Vera Stein, a Swiss journalist who was a cousin of Vladimir Nabakov, and a younger female relative of Chaim Weizmann, a scientist in her own right. Only one Sabra among the lot.

When we arrived Ben-Gurion was busy working out with Eytan's help a birthday telegram to President Charles De Gaulle.

In making small talk with Paula Ben-Gurion, my luncheon partner, I complimented her on the absence of flies, whose presence in large numbers had spoiled many a prior visit for me to new settlements. Her reply: Fool — don't you realize they have nothing to eat here!

After lunch, Ben-Gurion took us on a tour of the neighborhood and showed us where he planned to build the science complex that would lead the way to the development of the Negev. There was nothing but sand as far as the eye could see except that Ben-Gurion saw more, the complex of buildings and the scientists who would be working there before long.

In mid-afternoon we flew in an army plane to Tel Aviv, and a car took me to Haifa so that I could spend the New Year with my relatives. A small country, with a big vision, knowing that it could count on the affection and support of Jews from other countries. No one could foresee the end of the effort but the beginning was indeed impressive.

As quoted earlier, Dr. Weizmann believed that the-about-to-be-established state of Israel needed a half century to get itself firmly established. The year 1988 marks the passage of four of the five decades. In the absence of cataclysmic developments, such as the outbreak of a major war or the loss of support of the U.S. government, Israel is well on its way to assuring its long-term survival, despite the hostility of its neighbors, internal dissensions, religious fanaticism, and the loss of its pioneering ethic.

9

In Search of Perspective

The thrust of this book has been to assess the multiple forces, internal and external, that have been altering the lives of American Jews during the twentieth century, more particularly during the period since World War II. When I wrote the *Agenda* in the late 1940s, I emphasized the following: the markedly reduced role of religious observance and respect for Jewish law and tradition; the declining proportion of the Jewish population that was affiliated with the synagogue and to whom regular participation on a weekly basis was important; the impoverished state of Jewish education as measured by the proportion of Jewish youngsters who attended Jewish schools, the amount and quality of the schooling they received, and the early age at which those who had been enrolled dropped out. My assessment also indicated that many Jews limited their affiliation to national organizations, which were primarily concerned with combating anti-Semitism, which consumed a disproportionate amount of money and energy, and which on balance would not prove effective, since most non-Jews would hold onto their prejudices and there was relatively little that Jews could do to alter them.

I noted that the establishment of the state of Israel in 1948 presented a major challenge to the long-established Zionist organizations, which henceforth would have to find a new rationale for their activities. I noted further the larger challenge that faced the millions of American Jews who had to define their position toward the new state and determine the extent to which they would become involved in helping it develop. The foregoing in broad brush is where I had come out in 1949 after having taken a hard look at the structure and functioning of Jewish organizations and the behavior of Jews in the United States shortly after the end of World War II.

As noted earlier, against a recorded history of 3,000 years, four decades represents only a little more than 1/100 of the recorded experience of the Jews, hardly long enough for definitive analysis and evaluation. But there is another measurement that must be considered: forty years is the approximate working life of most men in twentieth-century America. Since each individual's adult life-span continues to be about a half century, a forty-year period cannot be brushed aside as of little or no importance. While Jewish experience may best be evaluated in terms of centuries and even millennia, each individual Jew must locate himself or herself and one's changing experiences in terms of much briefer units of time, in decades and generations.

Let me begin this assessment of these four decades by some modification and corrections of the interpretations that I had earlier advanced in the *Agenda*. This beginning should serve as a reminder of the need for continuing caution and circumspection when offering new readings and interpretations of recent events. First, I believe that the strong trend to a thinning of religious belief and observance has continued apace. Although I did not allow for the explosive growth of the suburban synagogue-community center, my asumption that a steadily declining proportion of American Jews would be affiliated with congregations and participate in weekly services has not been contradicted by subsequent events. The sorry state of Jewish education, with some notable exceptions noted below, was likewise confirmed as the postwar decades unfolded.

The two major avenues where my anticipations were seriously awry related to the unique place that the new state of Israel came to enjoy in the hierarchy of values and commitments of American Jews; and the amazing decline in religious prejudice in the United States, particularly in the economic and social arenas, with the result that Jews confronted greatly expanded opportunities to establish themselves in most of the prestigious and high-income sectors of the American economy.

This search for perspective is not aimed at pinpointing the number of places and times where my original analysis was more or less confirmed by later events but will focus, rather, on selected developments that I had initially ignored or had underestimated. No significance attaches to the order in which the unexpected developments are reviewed below. But each of the "happenings" singled out for inspection has the potential for more than transitory influence on shaping the American Jewish experience in the decades and generations that lie ahead.

The first new dominant force that we shall look at is the new vitality of the Orthodox. Both the post-World War II immigration of the Hasidim from Eastern Europe and the coming of age of the new generation of native American Orthodox are significant and unexpected developments. Although their numbers are relatively small, the intensity of their

"Jewishness" cannot be minimized. To begin with, the neo-Orthodox offspring of American parentage are proof that one can be a college or university graduate, a successful professional or businessperson, and still live a committed Jewish life with all of the commandments that are built into such a belief-structure and lifestyle.

Among the major contributions of the neo-Orthodox has been the impetus that both the native-born and the Hasidic immigrants have provided for the establishment and expansion of all-day schools and Talmudic academies, the latter concentrating on extended study of rabbinic texts by self-selected groups of young men. We called attention earlier to the significant influence that the Orthodox exert through sending considerable numbers of their young people to Israel for additional years of study and the financial contributions they are making to building and strengthening their institutions in the Holy Land. There are many non-Orthodox Jews in Israel and the United States who view these actions as dysfunctional because they see the Orthodox as contributing to the exacerbation of religious tensions in Israel. However, not all or even most of the sons and daughters of American Orthodox families who go on extended study missions to Israel get involved in street brawls or are seeking to turn the state into a theocracy. Many want to live the type of Jewish life that has commended itself to their parents and themselves and they turn their backs on exacerbating the political struggle.

In the United States, the neo-Orthodox must also be seen as a potent force pushing, pulling, propelling many federations to look anew at their previously insignificant financing for Jewish education. While the non-Orthodox congregational leadership has played an important role in persuading local federations to reassess their budgeting with an aim of allocating more funds for Jewish education, the enlarged federation support for Jewish schools has surely been in part responsive to the strident demands of the Orthodox.

Though the data leave much to be desired, casual inspection of sidewalk traffic in neighborhoods where large numbers of the Orthodox reside suggests that many young couples take the biblical injunction to "increase and multiply" literally. Many families can be seen out for a walk with three, four, or five young children in tow. And the demographic issue must be given due attention in assessing the future of the Jews both in the United States and in Israel. The Orthodox take their commitments seriously, including a personal responsibility to see that the Jews do not die out.

There are several closely related developments bearing on Jewish educational activities beyond the boundaries of the Orthodox that warrant review and assessment. The first relates to the growing involvement of the

Conservative movement in the establishment of Jewish day schools and a modest move in the same direction by a limited number of Reform congregations. The impetus for this non-Orthodox interest in and furtherance of day schools reflects a combination of forces positive and negative: a growing dissatisfaction with the inadequacies of both the afternoon Hebrew school and the Sunday school; the deterioration of many urban public educational systems as a consequence of large-scale in-migration of low-income minority groups, and the growing acceptance on the part of many Americanized Jewish families that there is no special risk to sending their children to a Jewish day school. Even if the children attend a parochial school, they can grow up to become well-integrated members of the larger community.

Closely related, but still distinguishable, are other developments that have strengthened the educational experiences of many Jewish children and young adults. An important innovation has been the Camp Ramah initiative under the auspices of the Conservative movement, which provides intensive Jewish exposures and experiences for many young people during their two-month summer vacation. This experience, when repeated for a number of summers, often assures that their values and lifestyles will be strongly influenced by their prior adolescent experiences.

Both the Conservative and the Reform movements began to experiment with weekend retreats and other conferencing techniques for young leaders aimed at increasing the opportunities for Jewish experiences and learning by interested and involved young people. But the most striking educational development has taken place in colleges and universities with the introduction and proliferation of offerings in Judaica. In the pre-World War II era there were a handful of Jews who held faculty positions at leading universities whose field of specialization was Judaica or cognate areas such as Near Eastern studies: David Blondheim at Johns Hopkins, Isaac Husik and Abraham Speiser at the University of Pennsylvania, Salo Baron at Columbia, and Harry A. Wolfson at Harvard. The founding members (1918) of the American Academy of Jewish Research and most of the members at the outbreak of World War II were on the faculties of the leading Jewish institutions, primarily Jewish Theological Seminary, Hebrew Union College, Jewish Institute of Religion, Dropsie College, and the Yeshiva. By the mid-1980s only about half of the membership of the American Academy of Jewish Research was based at the leading Jewish institutions: the other half included, among others, faculty members from the University of California, both UCLA and Berkeley; Stanford; Columbia; Texas Christian University; Rutgers; Indiana; Boston University; University of Chicago; Pennsylvania; Iowa; New York University; Yale; Institute of Advanced Studies; Brown; University of

Texas; Harvard. Although Brandeis, which has several fellows in the academy, is a secular institution, it has, from its establishment, emphasized the cultivation of Jewish studies.

Judaism, in its Spring 1986 issue, presented no fewer than eight articles on the subject of "Jewish Studies in the Universities: A Balance Sheet," written by informed insiders. The editor, Robert Gordis, notes in his introduction that "there are nearly a thousand members in the Association for Jewish Studies, the professional organization in the field, and several hundred schools offer programs of greater or lesser scope in the area." While quantitative criteria have limited utility in illuminating complex aspects of Jewish experience such as the values and meanings that are embedded in this proliferation of offerings of Judaica in institutions of higher learning, they are useful in underscoring a few simple facts and trends. The first unequivocal fact is that a large number of leading colleges and universities have belatedly come to recognize the legitimacy of Judaic studies within the panoply of their curriculum offerings.

Some of the more important facets of this explosive growth to which the writers of *Judaism* drew attention include the continuing imbalance between an array of introductory survey courses and the restricted number of serious graduate offerings; the attraction of these offerings not only to Jewish but to many non-Jewish students; the abysmal preparation of most Jewish students in reading Hebrew texts, even those with many years of preparatory instruction; the unrealizable expectations of many Jewish parents and Jewish leaders who expect such courses to provide the content and the motivation for Jewish identification; the relative thinness of faculty resources, which has resulted in appointments running far ahead of qualified individuals; the frequency with which these courses suffer from a lack of breadth or depth.

But these and still other criticisms and shortcomings cannot negate the significance of this seeding of Judaic studies in institutions of higher learning, which has led to expanded contributions and strengthened potential for creative Jewish scholarship. This unexpected and large-scale development came largely out of the blue, which should serve as a reminder and a warning that even well-informed scholars and leaders in the Jewish world are likely to be upstaged by events that cannot be foreseen.

From this brief review of the Jewish day school and the place of Jewish studies in higher education, let us turn to a fourth dominant force in American Jewish life. Ever since the Jewish Agency was organized in 1929, the ranks of American Jews had begun to close behind those who advocated active assistance to building up the homeland. This trend was reaffirmed and strengthened in 1942 when representatives of American Jewry went on record to support at war's end the creation of an independent Jewish state. The opportunities and dangers that the embryonic state would face over the following decades — from the mass absorption of the Jewish refugees from the DP camps and from the Muslim countries, to beating back its enemies in 1956, 1967, and 1973, to the rescue and absorption of a large segment of Ethiopian Jews — called forth the enthusiasm and support of ever larger numbers of American Jews.

There are several dimensions of the relations between American Jews and Israel that warrant inspection. The first is the small number of American Jews who were willing to give *aliyah* a trial. Even the committed Zionists did not become settlers in the new state. One can argue that the Jewish Agency, which had responsibility for encouraging settlement in Israel, was not judicious in its choice of emissaries, but I doubt that even the most skilled recruiters would have been successful. Resettlement in Israel had never been an integral part of American Zionist ideology, and when the state became a reality, the weak ideological underpinnings were further strained by the expanded opportunities for Jews in the United States, which made emigration even less attractive.

The growing affluence of American Jews and the vast improvements in air travel enabled an ever larger proportion of Jews to visit Israel. The estimate made in the mid-1980s is that approximately two of every five American Jews have visited Israel at least once.

The senior Israeli leadership, including prime ministers, other high-ranking government officials, senior military, members of the Knesset, the diplomatic corps, and still others, have made frequent visits to America, during which they have held small, large, and occasionally mammoth meetings with Jewish groups in all of the nation's large cities and on occasion also in smaller communities. They took the time and trouble to explain to their co-religionists in America the immensity and urgency of the problems that Israel faces and will continue to face and elicited the ongoing involvement and support of those whom they addressed.

Among the striking successes that the Israelis achieved in these continuing dialogues and fund-raising efforts were the successful launching and continuation of the campaign to sell Israeli bonds to American Jews and also to friendly organizations such as trade unions for their pension funds and other investments. The most interesting aspects of the Israeli-American connection are the many ways in which the development of the new state gave new meaning, direction, and depth to the lives of many American Jews. To overstate the case: for great numbers for whom affiliation had attenuated to the point where they attended services on the High Holy Days and made an annual contribution to their federations, the difficulties, struggles, and victories of Israel provided a new focus and meaning to their Jewish existence. Israel provided at least a partial substitute for what earlier generations had found in religious beliefs and traditional observances.

The response of American Jews was by no means limited to a passive role of watching and cheering from the sidelines, and it went considerably beyond the activities bounded by fund-raising, important activity as this has been and continues to be. The critical role of the U.S. government in the development of Palestine was first revealed in the weeks before the issuance of the Balfour Declaration in World War I, which might never have seen the light of day except for the desire of His Majesty's government to humor President Woodrow Wilson, whose support was critical to the survival of Britain. From that day to this, the role of the U.S. government in the establishment and the strengthening of the state of Israel has matured to a point where the American-Israeli connection has begun to approximate the closeness of United States relations to its NATO (North Atlantic Treaty Organization) allies and to South Korea and Australia.

In light of the ways in which U.S. foreign policy is determined, by pulling and tugging among the White House, the Departments of State and Defense, the Congress, and organized interest groups and public opinion, American Jews have had their work cut out for them once they decided that tightening the bonds between the United States and Israel stood at the very top of their agenda.

I had breakfast with Abba Eban and Reuven Shiloah in Washington on the day that Nasser announced that he would seek arms from Eastern Europe. My suggestion to the ambassador and his minister was as simple as it proved at the time to be impractical: explain to the press, the public, and the politicians that the Israeli-Egyptian confrontation was only a sideshow compared to the underlying and unremitting struggle between the United States and the USSR for control of strategic areas such as the Middle East. The Israeli representatives acknowledged that my analysis had much to commend it, but as representatives of a sovereign state, they could not tell the United States government how to interpret and respond to Nasser's diplomatic tour de force.

With the passage of time, the United States and Israel moved to joint response to aggressive actions in the area. In 1970, at the request of the United States, the Israelis moved troops to the Syrian-Jordanian border to send a message to Syria, an ally of the USSR, not to order its army into Jordan. In subsequent years closer relations have been established between Israel and the United States on all major political, intelligence, and military developments in the area.

While most U.S. strategists have come to look upon Israel as this country's most potent and dependable ally in the unstable Middle East, particularly since the overthrow of the shah in Iran, the decision-makers in Washington also understand the extent to which such a friendly, cooperative policy has the active support of the overwhelming proportion of American Jews and a large sector of the non-Jewish population.

Although there have been times when Israel incurred major losses in American public opinion, concomitant to its invasion and occupation of Lebanon — not only among the Christian majority, but among significant groups of Jews — it has been able to recoup much of these losses after the withdrawal of its troops from Lebanon and the resignation of Menachem Begin as prime minister.

A key instrument for the continuing support in Washington of a broad-based constructive policy toward Israel has been the well-organized American Israel Public Affairs Committee (AIPAC), which has come to play an ever larger role in making sure of the support for Israel in both the Senate and the House, and in the key congressional committees such as Appropriations, Armed Services, and Foreign Affairs. A significant number of mutual-support alignments have been worked out between members of Congress who come from districts and states with relatively large and concerned Jewish constituents who place a high value on pro-Israel policies and members from districts and states with few Jews who need their colleagues' support for farm, public works, and other local interests.

The careful and continuing cultivation of strong congressional support also helps to restrain the introduction and execution of administrative rules and regulations that might have a deleterious effect on Israel. Only rarely, as in the case of AWACS, did two presidents (Carter and Reagan) enter into and carry through a fight for the sale to Saudi Arabia in the face of strong congressional opposition. In Washington, key political groups are likely to make minor concessions in order to win larger objectives. In the total scheme of things, Israeli requests for continuing assistance have been easier to meet in the 1980s because of the breadth and depth of congressional support, aided and abetted by a generally well-inclined White House and Department of State.

The focused attention of so much Jewish interest and effort on Israel has been a major factor in energizing the ways in which activist groups relate to politics, especially at the national level. The Jewish leadership long ago left behind the tactics of the pre-World War II era when its spokesmen relied on their personal relations with those in positions of power to seek their intercession on behalf of overseas Jews who were at risk. Taking a leaf from the more successful interest groups, particularly big business, the farm bloc, and veterans' organizations, the Jews have learned the game of supporting their friends and weakening their opponents — with support of Israel as the litmus test.

While there are many ethnic groups in the United States that are concerned from time to time about their countries of origin and seek to influence Washington policy in a particular direction — consider the Irish, the Greeks, the Eastern Europeans whose homelands are dominated by the USSR — American Jews are more deeply and surely more continuously involved in helping the young state of Israel.

We have now inspected four positive forces that have emerged with unexpected strength in the post-World War II era and that have begun to reshape parts if not the whole of the Jewish experience in the United States: the rise of neo-Orthodoxy; the Jewish day school; Jewish courses at colleges and universities; and the dominating role that the state of Israel has come to play in eliciting the ongoing support and involvement of large sections of American Jewry.

There remain two additional transforming forces that warrant attention and analysis. Each is primarily a post-World War II phenomenon: the changing role of women in Jewish organizations, and the consequences of the lowering and the removal of religious prejudice in U.S. society with particular emphasis on the impact of these changes on marriage patterns.

Led by the most successful of all organized Jewish women's groups, Hadassah, which had its beginnings prior to World War I, a number of large national women's organizations were established in the ensuing decades, including those affiliated with the Reform and Conservative movements, ORT, and the Jewish Welfare Board, among others. In addition, each of the large federations as well as local synagogues, hospitals, and other eleemosynary organizations have benefited from the continuing involvement of a women's auxiliary.

Until recently, women were not selected for the top positions in the major national organizations and had to settle for leading their own exclusively female organizations. But that has now begun to change in large measure as the result of the lowering of sex barriers throughout the whole of American society.

Hadassah warrants some further brief comments because of the light that it sheds on the changing relations of organized Jewish efforts in the United States on behalf of the Yishuv and the state of Israel. First of all, Hadassah, from the outset, set itself a defined program area — health, primarily the delivery of health services. In the aftermath of the Holocaust it broadened its program to include special efforts directed to the resettlement and integration of surviving children — Youth *Aliyah* — in Israel. With the growth of the city of Jerusalem and the Hebrew University,

Hadassah broadened considerably the basis of its support for its flagship hospital, which has become the most important medical center in the Middle East. Its transfer of funds from the United States in 1986 for the support of its Israeli programs totaled $30,300,000. Despite this high level of support, most of which goes to its medical center in Jerusalem, the relationship between Hadassah and the Israeli government has become strained because, among other reasons, Hadassah is no longer in a position to cover all or even most of the operating costs of its facilities, while it still seeks to determine their scale, scope, and quality. While this sponsor-Israeli government tension is by no means limited to Hadassah and in fact is present in all institutions that depend for a significant part of their funding on American and other friends abroad, it presents a clear case of fiscal responsibility versus operational control.

While the women of Hadassah contributed a great deal to organizing and motivating large numbers of middle-class Jewish women (and their husbands) in the United States on behalf of Palestine and later Israel, it is by no means the only women's organization that left its mark on Jewish life. ORT has a strong women's contingent; in fact most of the fundraising in the United States for ORT's vocational school system in Israel and in the many countries in Europe and Latin America is done by women. On the domestic front, organized Jewish women have helped to carry the message of both the Reform and the Conservative movements at local and national levels. And there are other areas, such as the Jewish Welfare Board, where women provide support services to Jews in the Armed Services.

American Jewish women have been the basic guardians of home-based traditions; they have usually played a prominent part in overseeing the religious instruction of their children; they have had fewer conflicts in attending weekly synagogal services. It is therefore not surprising that they finally sought to enter the training seminaries for rabbis with the goal of achieving ordination.

The Reform and Reconstructionist movements responded first to the idea of seminary training for women, in the 1970s. The faculty of the Jewish Theological Seminary initially presented the proposal (1979), and after several years of additional discussions, lobbying, and politics, the proposal with Chancellor Gerson Cohen in the lead was carried in 1983. It appears that the decision to ordain women was passed because the majority of the leaders and members of the Conservative movement could no longer rationalize their exclusion. The proponents recognized that ordination of women could be viewed as a major break with tradition, one that would not be accepted by those who respect and live by the Halachah. But the vast majority of the membership of Conservative synagogues were no longer living in accordance with law and tradition. It seemed to the proponents of ordination that the price of continued exclusion of women was too high in a community in which the future of Judaism depends on the interest and involvement of individuals who participate voluntarily.

The first fall-out of the decision of the Conservative movement to ordain women was the dissolution of the joint body, which had previously included the Orthodox, in selecting chaplains for the Armed Services. The Orthodox, doctrinally opposed to the ordination of women, withdrew from the cooperative arrangement and each of the movements will henceforth nominate its own chaplains. The move to the ordination of women had further widened the breach between the Orthodox rabbinate in Israel and the non-Orthodox rabbis in the United States, which, as we shall see in the concluding chapter, has serious ramifications for the ongoing relationship between Israel and American Jews.

Finally, it remains to be seen whether the ordination of women rabbis will lead, in fact as well as in theory, to a significant broadening and deepening of the leadership cadre among American Jews, which will be reflected in the attraction/retention of greatly enlarged numbers of affiliated and participating Jews. It may yet turn out that the rationale that underlay the campaign for female ordination to invigorate contemporary Judaism in the United States proved to be not as strong as its supporters maintained.

As a small, often as a very small, minority living amidst hostile populations in the Diaspora, Jews have long been acutely aware of what can best be described as their perpetual vulnerability. Accordingly one of the major preventive measures they adopted to reduce their vulnerability was to erect rigid barriers to intermarriage between Jew and non-Jew. Since conversion was seldom an option that the non-Jewish partner would consider, intermarriage had the inevitable consequence of diminishing the Jewish population. Orthodox Jews sat *shiva*, that is, they said prayers for the dead when an offspring picked a non-Jewish spouse and conforming Jews broke off, at least in theory, all relations with those who married outside the faith.

The much lower level of religious prejudice in the United States since World War II, together with the broadened educational, occupational, and social opportunities available to American Jews, had the certain and inevitable consequence of a vast increase in their rate of intermarriage. The scattered data, based mostly on studies of middle-sized communities, suggests that the intermarriage rate is in the 25 percent range, possibly considerably higher among the most recent marriageable cohort. An extrapolation of current trends suggests that the rate is likely to continue to rise in the face of the following: the small number of Jews who continue to observe Jewish tradition and law; the large and growing numbers of unaffiliated Jews; the many Jewish women who are pursuing an active career, which increases the likelihood of their choosing a non-Jewish mate.

But we must not assume that the consequences of this high and probably still accelerating rate of intermarriage will have disastrous consequences for the Jewish community, resulting in a declining population, the more serious because of the low and declining Jewish birth rate.

There are several influences at work to suggest that the present high levels of intermarriage may prove less injurious than a simple projection of past experience might suggest. The first is the reduced attractiveness of marginally identified Jews who intermarry to become active members of a Christian denomination. In generations past, many Jews saw advantages to becoming converts to Christianity for economic or social reasons and intermarriage was often a first step. But in the late 1980s conversion to Christianity among Jews who intermarry is no longer significant.

A second point relates to Jewish law and tradition: the children of a Jewish mother are Jews even if their father is not. Hence as long as Jewish women who intermarry are interested in their children being brought up as Jews, there are no hurdles in the way, particularly if their husbands are neutral or supportive of such efforts.

The issue becomes more complicated when a Jewish man marries a non-Jewish woman. If she is willing to become converted, which has been made easier by the less stringent rules that the Reform rabbinate has instituted, the outcome can result in a net accretion to the Jewish population. Estimates suggest that the annual number of persons who become converted to Judaism is of the order of 10,000. The presumption is that both partners will want their children to be brought up as Jews.

The Reform movement has taken the radical step of declaring that Jewish identity can flow through the patriarchal as well as the matriarchal line, an approach that has as yet aroused little enthusiasm among the leaders of the Conservative branch.

The growing rate of intermarriage is part and parcel of the larger setting of a more open American society, reduced adherence to religious beliefs and practices, an attenuation of affiliation of both Jews and Christians with religious institutions, and the belief of many Jews that they can maintain their ties to the Jewish community even if they intermarry.

While many demographic analyses can be cited to support one or another conclusion of the currently high intermarriage rate, probably the most sensible interim assessment would consider it a phenomenon closely related to the growing number of nonaffiliated Jews. The partners of many marriages in which both are Jewish by birth have no active affiliation with the Jewish community. It is clear that a significant proportion of those who intermarry continue to be involved in Jewish life and affairs. The generational consequences for the children of nonaffiliated Jewish couples as distinct from the children of mixed marriages are not yet known. The differences may not prove to be significant.

Now that we have reviewed the six dominant new forces contributing to the restructuring of Jewish life in the United States in recent decades, I find it necessary to indicate, at least briefly, my personal assessment of the long-term significance of each.

The rise of neo-Orthodoxy is truly puzzling. I have no question that small numbers of Jews will always opt to give first priority to ritual observance, but it is hard for me to believe that the recent renaissance of Orthodoxy has a bright future in our increasingly secular culture except for the small numbers of the totally committed. But then one must remember that Judaism has long been shaped and reshaped by small cadres of devoted and dedicated adherents, which means that the Orthodox cannot be dismissed as nothing more than a fringe group.

In retrospect it strikes me as more than a little surprising that I never seriously entertained sending any of my three children to a Jewish day school even though two of them had to be removed from unsatisfactory public schools and transferred to private schools. I recall some strenuous arguments with my friend Arthur H. L. Rubin, Mordecai Kaplan's nephew and an associate of Robert Hutchins of the University of Chicago, who was an early enthusiast for Jewish day schools. He had a simple and straightforward position: the only prospect for a reasonable, educated Jewish laity was one whose members had the benefit of eight or preferably twelve years of Jewish education, together with a superior secular education. I have difficulty in recalling the specifics of my opposition, but I suspect that it rested on the risks entailed by enforced separatism, a risk that I would no longer consider relevant.

The blossoming of Judaica at U.S. institutions of higher learning cannot be seen as other than a boon, for it provides a new and powerful stimulus for the broadening and deepening of Jewish studies, which have long been the most creative factor in Jewish survival. Whether such studies, distant and divorced from active Jewish communal life, will have the same leverage as Jewish scholarship in the past is questionable, but they will surely contribute to the expansion of better-educated leadership and lay members.

As noted earlier, I am strongly of the belief that Israel has come to be the dominant factor in the life of the American Jewish community and the principal source of reinforced identification for millions of American Jews. The open issue is whether and to what extent this new and close relationship that developed after World War II will be eroded by the passage of time, conflicts over Jewish ethical and political objectives, and still other sources of disagreement and conflict. It would be indeed surprising if some of the enthusiasm of the last decades did not evaporate with the passage of time and as a result of growing disagreements if not conflicts. But it would be even more surprising if the love of Zion, a mainstay of 2,000 years of Jews in the Diaspora, were to be eroded now that the state has been reestablished.

The enlarged role for women in Jewish synagogal and community life should prove to be a source of strength and a contribution to broadening and deepening the leadership cadre even if it falls short, possibly far short, of the expectations of the more enthusiastic feminists and their male supporters. But this new and unanticipated development must be viewed as a source of strength for a community suffering many losses from the uninterested and the unaffiliated.

Finally, the threat of a high and possibly still higher rate of intermarriage is not to be taken lightly in an environment in which there is less and less pressure from the outside on Jews to remain actively involved in the Jewish community. The only encouragement that can be extracted from the experience of the last decades is that a significant minority of the marriages that take place between a Jew and a non-Jew results in the conversion of the latter, which generally assures that the children will be brought up as Jews and accept as adults their Jewish identity. But it would be Pollyannaish to ignore the risks to the American Jewish community that result from the continuing high rate of intermarriage, particularly in the face of the low birth rate characteristic of most Jewish couples, the Orthodox alone excepted.

Our search for perspective has uncovered not one but six powerful factors acting on and interacting with each other to alter the structures and lifestyles of American Jews. Whether these powerful factors will, on balance, turn out to be positive or negative on the survival and vitality of the Jewish community in the United States of the next century remains unclear. In the concluding chapter we shall probe further.

10

The Future Will Tell

Shortly before I began to write this book, I encountered Ismar Schorsch, then newly appointed as chancellor of the Jewish Theological Seminary, near the Columbia campus and told him briefly what I was up to. He asked where I was coming out, and to his surprise as well as my own I indicated that the answer was still to be determined. For one who usually outlines his last chapter first, I began to reflect on what lay back of this deviation from my norm.

I undertook to write this book because I sought clarity. I was uncertain about how the many trends and countertrends in the American Jewish community were to be assessed. In addition, I had no way of tying together current developments on the American Jewish scene to the centuries of Diaspora experience; and I had more questions than answers in projecting the next stages of American Jewry in the face of the reality of the state of Israel, which is exercising major influence on the present and presumably the future of American Jews.

To add to the foregoing uncertainties, I was aware of the need for an analysis about the future trends in the United States, which had become home to the largest Jewish community in the history of the Jews, since these trends would assuredly affect, if not determine, the direction of Jewish life in the future just as the earlier development of the nation had done so much to shape the evolution of American Jewry.

As I neared the end of my writing, I became more aware of the inherent difficulties that constrain every analyst of the changing Jewish scene—the inevitability that one's analysis is heavily conditioned by one's point of departure and personal philosophy. To illustrate: one of my good friends on the West Coast reported in the summer of 1986 the following snippets of a conversation. A colleague went to visit Sidney Hook, in Palo Alto, who was exercised by recent reports that his old friend Daniel Bell was becoming ever more "religiously" oriented. Irrespective of whether Bell in fact was becoming more religious, the nature of Hook's concern highlights the headlock that the analyst's preconceptions exercise over his analysis.

While much is made of generational shifts, including a movement back toward tradition and religious observance among the third and fourth generations of American Jews whose parents had eliminated all or most Jewish content from their lives, these reversals should not be exaggerated. In a highly competitive American society, only an occasional college student or graduate is likely to reorder his or her values and practices in order to make a major investment in studying Jewish history, literature, and ethics; to acquire even a minimum command of Hebrew; or to join a synagogue and observe traditions and ceremonials that have provided the structure for the lives of practicing Jews over the past two millennia. Of course, a small minority continues to follow the route of tradition. But many more go the other way and distance themselves from their Jewish inheritance.

The following brief account of the Jewish content of the lives of five generations of Ginzbergs in the twentieth century will help to flesh out this critical point. My paternal grandfather, at the age of seventy, stood during an eight-hour train ride from Bad Homburg to Amsterdam because his wife, who was ailing, needed the comfort of second-class travel. He refused to sit down because of his uncertainty whether the seat was *shatnis*, a prohibited admixture of flax and wool. His mother, my great grandmother, had moved some years earlier from Lithuania to Holland to live in his household (he was her only child), but after five years, at the age of ninety, she returned to Kovno because she did not feel that she could rely on the ritual observance in Amsterdam.

My father was an observant Jew but was not considered to be so by members of the Orthodox community: he put on a yarmulka only at prayer time and while studying religious texts; he ate fish in restaurants; he fasted only on Yom Kippur and a half day on Tishabov.

Even when my children were growing up, our ceremonial observance at home was marginal; synagogue attendance was infrequent, and both Sabbath observance and the dietary laws were not part of our regimen. The first marriage among my three children was between my youngest daughter and a young man of American-Italian background whose basic schooling had been in a Jesuit institution. The marriage ceremony was performed by a Reform rabbi with whom the young people had studied for several months.

This snapshot recapitulation of the erosion of "Jewish capital" within less than a single century should be a powerful reminder that in matters of religious observance, capital consumption is much more likely than capital accumulation.

The optimists among observers of the contemporary Jewish scene in the United States would argue that the foregoing illustration proves little. Jews must adapt to the dominant culture of which they are a part, and one should not have expected that the ghetto life of East European Jewry could have been transferred, taken root, and survived in a secular, technologic society such as that of the United States in the twentieth century. Admitted — but what are the bases for optimism about the ability of U.S. Jews to find effective substitutes for the capital they have lost?

The conventional answers fall under several rubrics. First, the desire of many (possibly most) Jews to retain an active affiliation with the Jewish community, at least during the years when they are rearing their children. Second, their selective observance of customs and traditions from lighting candles on Friday evening, the celebration of Hanukkah and Passover, synagogue attendance on the High Holy Days, and observing ritual practices at the time of confirmation, marriage, male births (circumcision), and death. The third reinforcement to the optimists' scaffolding relates to the active support by American Jews for a large array of local, national, and international Jewish organizations, which attest to their continuing identification with their brethren at home and abroad.

Finally, there is the powerful anchorage provided by the state of Israel, the home of over 3 million Jews, the second largest extant Jewish community. No one who has ever visited Jerusalem will fail to appreciate the overwhelming continuity of Jewish experience. And the daily newspaper is a constant reminder that Israel has an importance many times greater than its modest population and small territory.

Some among the optimists add an additional factor. They draw attention to the endemic nature of anti-Semitism in the United States and in the rest of the world, and in the view of such a latent threat no Jewish group can fail to remain vigilant so that it can take early action to thwart its enemies.

The basis for a pessimistic appraisal starts from a different reading of each of the foregoing trends. First, while the pessimists would acknowledge that there is an attenuated level of group adherence to tradition and ceremonial activities, they would also emphasize the diminishing number of Jews who are able to read Hebrew and who are interested in living an active Jewish life. When we take account of the large numbers of Jewish youth who receive at best a spotty Jewish education, the nonreligiously oriented are poorly positioned to deepen their knowledge and understanding of their tradition. Jews who do not pray and Jews who do not have any knowledge in depth of the Jewish past will not be able to give their children the building blocks out of which a Jewish future can be fashioned and made secure.

Second, what about the breadth and depth of the Jewish infrastructure in the United States? Surely that attests to the presence of a strong life-force. There is no need to adopt a hypercritical view of the federation movement and the significant number of local, national, and international organizations, each of which is dedicated to furthering one or another aspect of Jewish life: assisting poor Jews in need, supporting Jewish cultural activities, funding Jewish educational institutions, employing staffs that monitor anti-Semitism, and above all helping the new state of Israel to meet its defense and development needs.

The existence of such a large number of organizations dedicated to the furtherance of Jewish objectives must surely be read as evidence of the desire of many Jews to keep actively affiliated with the Jewish community. But as Daniel J. Elazar pointed out in his insightful book *Community and Polity: The Organizational Dynamics of American Jewry* (1976), a relatively small number of concerned, interested, and affluent Jews (with the assistance of a bureaucracy) has provided most of the leadership. With the exceptions of Hadassah, Women's ORT, and a few other organizations, the membership is largely inert except when it comes to fund-raising activities and check-writing. Many synagogues reflect the same dichotomous structure between a small number of activists and a largely passive membership that attends mostly on the High Holy Days.

Thirdly the continuing support of American Jews for Israel must be seen as a strongly affirmative stance. Once again the answer is not unequivocal but it does invite more careful appraisal. The data point to at least one ominous trend: the proportion of American Jews who contribute to Israel and Israeli institutions is declining. Moreover, while it is impressive that two of every five Jews have visited Israel at least once, that statistic also reveals that three out of five have never visited the state, in many cases not because they cannot afford to travel but because they have not been sufficiently interested to do so.

The excitement that attached to the years immediately preceding the emergence of the state and the many crises that it confronted during its early years are not part of the consciousness of the younger generation. With the passage of time it will become even dimmer as successive generations of parents will be unable to transmit to their children any firsthand knowledge of this overriding event in modern Jewish history.

The erosion is also occurring with respect to the Holocaust despite the efforts of the Holocaust survivors, scholars, and writers, and the special efforts that the Israeli government made at the Adolf Eichmann trial to remind those who knew and to instruct those who were uninformed about the magnitude of the evil that had befallen modern Jewry. It is more than a generation since the verdict on Eichmann was handed down in Jerusalem.

Each Jew has to resolve the meaning of the Holocaust individually. Faced with the option of coming into closer contact with the physical environment in which the mass exterminations were carried out, I have avoided visiting any of the concentration camps. I still have to go to visit Yad Vashem in Jerusalem. I have also limited my reading in the Holocaust literature. I have carefully avoided selecting movies or attending plays in which the "extermination theme" is central or even peripheral.

I have made a deliberate effort to keep my distance from all exposures to an evil unmatched in the long record of man's inhumanity to man. And I have not read widely or deeply in the theological tracts that have sought to find answers to the unanswerable question: Where was God and why did he not answer when his children called on him in the hour of their desperation? Despite my efforts to distance myself, the Holocaust has been the overriding experience of my adult years in the shaping and reshaping of my views of Jews and Judaism both in the Diaspora and in Israel.

The Holocaust has, however, been more an upsetting tale than a living experience to American Jews, with the exception of the U.S. Jewish soldiers and officers who had entered the concentration camps in the last days of the war. And time has a way of making the unexperienced unreal until all linkages to the event, especially to events of unparalleled evil, are weakened and obliterated.

The fourth arena where erosion is proceeding apace for American Jews is the future role of anti-Semitism as a force in American life. Since the end of World War II, anti-Semitism has receded on most fronts — religious, economic, social. But there have been a few reminders that the virus may be inactive rather than dead. Aside from small bands of neo-Nazis in the South, Midwest, and Northwest who have made trouble but who have been contained, certain attitudes and behavior continue to characterize significant sectors of the electorate. We called attention earlier to the disappointment of the Jewish defense agencies, which, after years of ecumenical associations with Protestant church leaders, discovered that most of the Christian leadership had little understanding of and less sympathy for the military vulnerability of the state of Israel or the importance of Israel to America and world Jewry. Non-Jews can always find reasons to tip the scales against Jews, and the unsolved problems of the Palestinians represent a counterweight to Israel's claims. But it requires more than a sensitivity to equity to equate the two.

In 1956 I paid a visit to the dean of the College of Cardinals in Rome,

Cardinal Eugène Tisserant, to discuss informally the attitude of the Vatican to Israel. He was a man of towering stature, great charm, and superb intellect. He welcomed me at his palace in Rome with the remark that he was especially honored to receive a visitor from the Holy Land on the Sabbath, a subtle reference to the fact that a mutual acquaintance had persuaded him not to visit his diocese that Saturday morning as was his wont, but also reminding me that I should not be traveling on the Sabbath.

Cardinal Tisserant told me that when he was still a member of the Deuxième Bureau he had traveled on muleback from Jerusalem to Damascus and he spoke of his continuing interest in the Middle East ever since that visit, which had occurred some years before the outbreak of World War I. He asked me for news about the United States, my views of Eisenhower and his administration as well as my assessment of the Israeli leadership and the problems of the new state. When I referred to Ben-Gurion he noted the great difficulties that the Vatican had in dealing with the new state. On the one hand, he referred to the extreme Orthodox who had no respect for some of the most important Christian shrines and who, if they had their way, would commit sacrilege. On the other hand, the cardinal said that Israel was the only government that had a minister of religion. To complicate matters, Prime Minister Ben-Gurion, Tisserant said, was an atheist, a statement that I questioned, suggesting that he could be better described as an agnostic or a deist, an interpretation that the cardinal was unwilling to accept. The cardinal pointed out that the Mother Church should not be expected to enter into relations with a nation, part of which denied the authenticity of Catholic beliefs and dogmas and whose leader was an atheist. I could see that the Vatican had left itself little room in which to maneuver.

The conversation then shifted to the problems of the church and Eastern Europe. Clearly the Vatican was strongly opposed to Communism but it had to pursue a long-range policy that might result over time in some amelioration of the conditions facing millions of its adherents. It could not afford to favor the strident pronouncements and policies that emanated from U.S. Secretary of State John Foster Dulles.

In discussing various religious and lay leaders in the United States, including key representatives of the Jewish minority, Cardinal Tisserant proved to me that the layman's view of the intelligence-gathering capabilities of the Vatican is correct. I was hard pressed to think of an American who was as well informed as the cardinal about the strengths and weaknesses of most of those whom we discussed. I came away from what was for me a most remarkable two-hour visit with one overriding conviction: every major organization or nation that had demonstrated the capacity to adjust and survive over long periods of time pursues its own priorities, in the hierarchy of which the problems of the Jews have a low, if any, place on its agenda. That was the major lesson of the Holocaust. Neither the United States under Roosevelt, nor Great Britain under Churchill, nor the Vatican under Pius XII found it necessary to take even minor risks to reduce, even if they could not stop, the slaughter.

To keep the record straight: the Holocaust surely played a large, probably the determining, role in Vatican Council II when it eliminated the charge of deicide in the Catholic belief structure, a momentous change in the relations between Catholics and Jews. And the present pope, John Paul II, by his words and actions has underlined the importance of the Holocaust in making the church more open to dialogue with the Jews.

The U.S. presidential election of 1980 saw a new development on the religious-political front. The Evangelicals, despite their southern fundamentalist origins and affinities, were wooed successfully by the Republican candidate and contributed significantly to his overwhelming victory. The price of this support was a series of promises by the candidate that the federal government would aim to protect or at a minimum not weaken, critical religious and moral values such as silent prayer in the schools, vouchers for private and parochial schools, antiabortion initiatives, and greater local autonomy that would enable conservative-minded citizens and communities to fashion their lives in accordance with their religious beliefs and moral convictions. The Evangelical leaders made it clear that the constitutional separation of church and state required reinterpretation to enable the United States to become once again the "Christian nation" that it had been in the early years after its entrance onto the stage of history.

The alliance between populist Christianity and populist Republicanism remained intact and President Ronald Reagan reaped the benefits therefrom in his reelection in 1984. Despite Evangelical support for the state of Israel and a pro-Israel administration in Washington, only a small minority of Jews voted Republican. Many more would have, had it not been for their belief that any narrowing of the separation of church and state was a major threat to their security.

The election campaign of 1984 was revealing in another regard. Jesse Jackson's unwillingness to reject the support of the overtly anti-Semitic black ideologist Louis Farrakan, who called Hitler a "great man" and who defined Judaism as a "gutter religion," was a potent reminder of the extent to which a section of the black community, represented in part by its better-educated, third-world supporters, saw U.S. Jews as a potential target. Friction between Jewish landlords, merchants, and civil servants, and black tenants, customers, and job-seekers was nothing new. What was new was the belief of some of the new black leadership that anti-Semitic appeals had a mobilizing potential in the political arena.

The opposition of many Jewish leaders and organizations to affirmative-action programs expressed in terms of quotas or guidelines was offered by some to explain the rise of the anti-Semitic black leader. But once again, as in the case of the unsolved problems of the Palestinians, the explanation is overly simplistic.

Let us remember: a high proportion of all white citizens, Democrats as well as Republicans, have lost their enthusiasm for affirmative action if they are not overtly hostile to it; and the predominant members of both parties couldn't care less about whether the Palestinians obtain a homeland. But selected black leaders have found both issues useful in their efforts to advance their own agendas, an effort that on occasion includes stirring up antagonism toward the Jews.

One of my intimate friends who has been closely associated with the Republican party leadership ever since the Eisenhower era dropped me a line during the 1980 presidential campaign to remind me that, since I was deeply interested in closer U.S.-Israeli relations, I should vote for Ronald Reagan, who was a strong supporter of what the Israelis had accomplished and would, if elected, continue to be a good friend of Israel. I did not question my friend's interpretation of Ronald Reagan's views and probable actions, but I have never believed in single-issue voting. While I believe that Reagan's record has fulfilled my friend's favorable forecast, I cannot overlook the fact that during the congressional debate about the sale of the AWACS to the Saudis, various representatives of the Reagan administration put forward the charge of dual loyalty against American Jews who were leading the fight to defeat the sale. Overtly and directly, they called attention to the fact that opponents of the sale were more interested in the security and welfare of Israel than of the United States. It was an ugly reminder of how quickly and easily anti-Semitism can be resurrected and used by politicians who find themselves in a tight spot.

While there was much to criticize about the Israeli invasion of Lebanon, especially the campaign north to Beirut, there is considerable evidence that the U.S. secretary of state, General Alexander Haig, was cognizant of and even encouraged the Israelis' actions. The critical analysis of the reporting by U.S. media—television, newspapers, magazines—leaves no question of the gross distortions of what occurred. One must read into this episode a low level of tolerance of the U.S. media for the behavior of the Israelis, if not outright anti-Semitism.

Much of the reporting may have been a belated expression of guilt for America's own much worse behavior in Vietnam, and some considerable part of the distortions may have been the result of television's emphasis on the dramatic rather than on the true. But these and still other explanations cannot obscure the widespread and deep hostility of most reporters and correspondents toward the Israelis, who were often likened to the Nazis and accused of genocide, language that reveals the depth of their anti-Semitic feelings.

The Bitburg episode, where President Reagan equated the victims of the Holocaust with their executioners and asked that both be honored in death, was a potent reminder of the gap in the feelings of friendly Christians and those of the Jewish minority who lost one-third of its members in Hitler's Final Solution. The president found himself in a constrained personal and diplomatic position, having promised Chancellor Helmut Kohl, a close ally, to visit a German military cemetery. But to Elie Wiesel, who pleaded with the president not to go through with his planned visit, the issue had transcendental significance — not to allow the world to forget or forgive the evil that the Holocaust represented. The world, at least the Western world, was shocked by the Holocaust, and for two generations its behavior has been affected by its recollection of the immensity of the evil that had been perpetrated on the innocent. But time passes, memories fade and, as we noted earlier, Jews are not likely to be placed high on the agenda of any nation other than Israel.

As of mid-1988 it is increasingly clear that the insurrection started by stone-throwing Palestinian youth in December 1987 and the repressive actions of the Israel Defense Forces have created new tensions both in Israel and among American Jews that will remain until some constructive resolution to the West Bank is found. The resolution will not prove easy given the heavy hand of history, ideology, security concerns of the Israelis, the yearnings for independence among the Palestinians, and disagreements among the principals and the other participants. But Israel cannot survive and flourish if it remains an occupying power; and the million and more Palestinians must have an opportunity to direct their own lives and fashion their own future.

Even though the outlines of a constructive resolution may still be hidden from view, the fact that more and more Israelis have come to recognize and accept the necessity sooner or later for a settlement is the best augury that a settlement will eventually be worked out.

I recall my shock when on my second visit to Israel, in 1956, during a tour under army auspices of the Arab villages in the neighborhood of Nablus, we stopped at the home of a village elder for tea. My escort, a captain in the Israel Defense Forces, sat in the living room of his commandeered host with his machine gun on his knee while the three of us exchanged pleasantries. The Israelis succeeded in the ensuing third of a century to work out a reasonable accommodation at least for the time being with the small Arab minority that did not relocate after the establishment of the state. But numbers count and there is no prospect of Israel's developing a comparable solution for the more than 1 million Palestinians whom it conquered in 1967. They need self-rule and political freedom, if under conditions of permanent neutrality, to work out their own destiny.

This abbreviated account of selected trends and events in the United States in the 1980s that point to potential developments that could threaten the future welfare of American Jews is not to be read as the inevitable recrudescence of anti-Semitism and even less its early return. But it is offered as a reminder to the many optimists who believe that American political tradition and social structure, with its diversity of ethnic groups, exclude the possibility of anti-Semitism becoming a potent force. My reading of the potential for anti-Semitism to become a significant factor on the U.S. political horizon depends at least in part on whether the future economic well-being and political influence of the United States in world affairs remains strong, or whether the country experiences recurrent crises and a relative loss of prestige and position that will precipitate domestic discontent and discord. I shall return to this theme again.

My former teacher and colleague, the distinguished sociologist, Robert Morrison MacIver, told his classes that the one safe generalization about demography is that every demographic forecast is likely to be proved wrong. Starting with Malthus, he was unable to identify any analyst whose theories did not fit his generalization. A half century and more has passed since I studied with MacIver but his generalization still appears to be valid in light of how far off the mark the neo-Malthusians, the Club of Rome, and other recent prophets of resource exhaustion have proved to be.

If demographic forecasts affecting the world or the major continents and nations have been seriously flawed, we must be doubly careful when it comes to forecasting the future population of Jews in the United States, Israel, or the world. In discussions with Ben-Gurion on one of my early visits to Israel, I was amazed when he told me that he looked forward to a Jewish population in Israel of 3 million or more. He did not pretend to know where they were coming from but he hoped that the USSR and the West, particularly the United States, would sooner or later be the source of significant increments. He was prescient about the former but wrong about the size of the inflow from the United States. He continued the demographic discussion on a more personal note. He wanted to know how many children we had and when I told him that we had three, he quickly added "good—see that one settles in Israel. That will be your contribution." A small quota but it is unlikely to be met.

Some years ago a demographic forecast was made of the future Jewish population of the United States, which suggested that the combined effects of a reproduction rate far below replacement, the disappearance of any sizable source of new immigrants, and the rising losses from intermarriage would result in the Jewish population's decline over successive decades from 5.5 million to a point where in the latter part of the twenty-first century it would be only a few hundred thousand.

This forecast had a psychological effect on the Jewish leadership and led to a considerable expansion of scholarly effort and community interest and investment in data collection and analyses of the key determinants of future population trends of American Jews. But there were difficulties facing such an enlarged effort: the U.S. Census has not collected information based on religion since the 1950s; there is no agreement among the leadership or the experts about the definition of a Jew; it is difficult to deal with respondent bias — how many offspring of parents who were Jewish have not been counted because the parents do not report themselves as Jews; the great difficulties and high costs involved in introducing reliable sample studies of Jews, particularly because of their heavy concentration in the three metropoli — New York, Los Angeles, and Chicago, which together account for about 40 percent of the total Jewish population in the United States.

The subsequent reanalysis of the dire prediction that American Jews would be almost extinct before the passage of another century is now considered to be fundamentally flawed. In its place are revised figures suggesting that the next half century is likely to see a decline of perhaps as much as 1 million or possibly slightly more in the number of U.S. Jews while the nation's population continues to grow so that the proportion of Jews in the total may shrink from 2.5 percent at this writing to not much more than half of that percentage, which the numbers-watchers translate into a potential heavy loss in the political arena.

The revised conclusions outlined above are also dependent on other inputs and assumptions about intermarriage and particularly the rearing of children of mixed marriages. As noted earlier, Jewish law stipulates that the children of a Jewish mother are Jews. But clearly in an open, secular state Jewish affiliation is not determining except within the organized Jewish community and frequently not even there, given the different practices of the different branches.

The issue becomes somewhat clarified when we take into account the number of non-Jewish spouses who convert to Judaism. The presumption is that they do so to satisfy their spouses that there will be no question that their children are Jewish. But that is the beginning, not the end of the matter, because the next question is whether the conversion is overseen by a rabbi who insists on full conformity to the laws of the Halachah or is directed by a Reform or a Conservative rabbi who bends some or many of the rules. In the latter instance, the religion of the convert and the children is far from settled: witness the position of the Israeli rabbinate, which recognizes as valid conversion of non-Jews only when it is carried out under the direction of an Orthodox rabbi.

The uncertainties about the present and future rates of intermarriage, conversion, and the rearing of children are only facets of the still larger issue of the likely trends affecting the identification and affiliation of the large and probably increasing number of Jews whose ancestry is not in dispute. If a significant proportion of Jews by birth have no ongoing affiliation with a synagogue, their children receive no Jewish education, and they do not contribute to their local federation or otherwise support Jewish organizations at home and abroad, what is the point of counting them as belonging to the Jewish community? The answer to this rhetorical question is twofold: some of their children, confused about their identity, may become affiliated in the future. And if events in the United States or abroad, particularly in Israel, take an ominous turn, the numbers who may activate or reactivate their membership in the Jewish community may increase substantially. Hence all meaningful demographic forecasts are highly contingent because they must make assumptions about both the yearnings and the desires of the individual as well as the quality of the American environment, the fate of Diaspora Jewry and, most important, the changing circumstances facing the state of Israel.

If we postulate that the U.S. environment will remain friendly and supportive as it has been since the end of World War II and if Israel's defense position and its economy become more secure, it would be a miracle if the number of currently nonaffiliated U.S. Jews did not grow until they represented a larger proportion of the total, which currently may approximate one-third. The combination of fewer and fewer linkages with their religion, history, tradition, literature, ethos, and ethics and of reduced pressures from the external environment almost certainly will increase the proportion of the nonaffiliated.

Careerism, social acceptance, the time that must be devoted to exercise and sports for health and pleasure — all leave little room for Jewish education, Jewish ceremonialism (Sabbath and holidays), and active participation in Jewish organizations.

The thrust of the foregoing is not that all or even most Jews will turn their backs on all forms of affiliation, but that those who have had little or no exposure and experience in childhood and adolescence to their rich tradition are unlikely to seek it out in adulthood and incorporate parts of it into their adult lifestyles.

Except for the relatively small numbers of dedicated Zionists and the much larger numbers who remained faithful to living as committed Jews in accordance with religious and legal precepts, we have the unequivocal testimony of history that previous efforts of European Jews to deal with their Jewishness from conversion, emancipation, or membership in a revolutionary party proved hollow — immigration to the United States and Israel alone excepted. But as suggested above, there are two major threats to the future of American Jews. The first comes from their continuing affluence and acceptance by the larger society; the second from a possible worsening in the environmental situation to a point where anti-Semitism might become a potent political platform for a significant political group in a period of severe economic and social disorder and distress. It would be fatuous at this late point in this analysis to offer a simplified explanation of the intensity and longevity of anti-Semitism in the Christian, Muslim, and Communist regions of the globe. But it might not be out of place to note in the present context that anti-Semitism has tended to grow and flourish in periods when nations face widespread domestic difficulties and disorders and when a scapegoat may ease the strain. Those in power or those making a play for power often seek to strengthen their position by evoking the slumbering dislike, envy, fear, and hatred of the masses toward the stranger, particularly the Jew, who has insisted on remaining apart.

One can identify two radically different views about the likely evolution in the role of Jews in the United States. The dominant view holds that the United States is different from other nations in so many basic respects, including its history, structure of government, openness to immigrants, respect for ethnic groups, absence of a state religion, and emphasis on individualism, that anti-Semitism has little or no prospect of becoming a potent political force. I find considerable merit in this view, but I want to reserve my position if the United States should enter upon a series of crises, political and economic, to which no ready solutions can be found. I am sufficiently uneasy about the United States and the world economy that I do not accept the theory that the Western world will continue to enjoy an ever higher standard of living with an adequate number of jobs for all who want and need to work. I hope and believe that such a scenario is probable, but I cannot rule out the alternative of disorder, crisis, and political upheavals. And if the latter should occur, it may result in all sorts of aberrant and destructive behavior, including a virulent form of anti-Semitism. But clearly the overwhelming majority of American Jews is not inclined to contemplate such a remote possibility and possible responses to it, including emigrating to Israel.

In my early visits to Israel, that is, in the 1950s and early 1960s, I was occasionally engaged in an argument by a concerned Zionist, particularly one who had been born in Eastern Europe, that I should consider making *aliyah* (immigrating) if not for my sake, then for the sake of my children. I was told that Jewish history pointed to the fact that it was only a matter of time before the U.S. environment would turn unfriendly if not hostile. I appreciated that this indeed was the lesson of Jewish history but I also understood that history need not, and often did not, continue in the same path even after having proceeded in a straight line for a long period. History will deliver its verdict about the anti-Semitic virus, but not until the twenty-first century or even later.

I can no longer hide behind additional hypotheses, analyses, and scenarios to delay my view of the denouement. My optimistic assumption is that the United States will avoid a major war and that it will not confront an economic catastrophe. Based on these assumptions, I shall now address the critical question about the future of American Jewry in the generations immediately ahead. Such a scenario forces one back to a consideration of the basic elements of Judaism without which all discussions about possible outcomes are stillborn. To avoid being boxed in on a narrow definition of the essence of Judaism, let us postulate that practicing or involved Jews must have some knowledge of Jewish history, some acquaintance with and respect for Jewish values, a sense of belonging to a people who, while remaining scattered over much of the earth, retain a love of Zion and a sense of obligation to ensure that this small people continue to contribute to making this a better world and, finally, see value in their own survival.

If the foregoing incorporates the basic elements of a creative Judaism, the next question is: How creative has American Judaism been in this century of turmoil and how creative is it likely to be in the generations ahead? As for the past, one can observe that, based on immigration primarily from Eastern Europe, it was possible for Jewish scholarship to sink roots in this new land. Further, the seminaries were able to train a large number of rabbis who helped the newcomers adapt their inherited beliefs and practices to the new environment, which contributed to an effective if difficult transplantation. Taking a lead from their Christian neighbors, the new Jewish immigrants outdid the natives in building voluntary organizations across a wide front — immigrant absorption, health, welfare, defense activities and, since World War II, agencies committed to the large-scale support of Israel.

While the existence of a highly diversified and well-financed infrastructure of voluntary organizations may be a foundation stone for a vital and creative Judaism in the United States, it does not assure a meaningful, constructive, and creative participation for large numbers of Jews. A closer view reveals that the organizational complex has a more limited reach: it provides opportunities for a relatively small leadership group, it gives a generally competent bureaucracy useful jobs and career opportunities, and it provides a minimum level of affiliation for sizable numbers of contributors.

If outcomes rather than structures are used to measure accomplishment and potential, how does one assess the state of contemporary American Jewry and, equally important, what are the probable lines of its development over the next decades? One way to explore this critical question is to identify the areas of present and potential Jewish creativity and to estimate whether the current and prospective forces are likely to have a positive, neutral, or negative effect on the future creativity of American Judaism.

We identified earlier the existence of a small Orthodox minority who are living and will continue to live a Jewish life in accordance with the Halachah. Their children receive a thorough Jewish education, and a significant number of their young men with scholarly interests continue into adulthood their study of the Talmud and other basic texts. With the exception of the extremists, these committed Orthodox have close bonds to Israel and many personal and institutional linkages, which lead many of their young people to pursue extended study missions in the Holy Land.

So far so good. This committed Orthodox minority, in addition to being the living guardians of the tradition, have made a significant contribution to American Jews through their aggressive efforts to build day schools, in which effort they have had considerable success and are likely to have more. But their potential for influencing the vast majority of their co-religionists, who give no evidence of wanting to take on the heavy burden of Jewish law and to order their lives in accordance with its dictates, is limited. Further, it is far from clear that the Orthodox community will be able to produce the scholars and the leaders it will require for its own survival and growth, and it is even less clear that they will be able to attract and remold significant numbers who are currently outside its fold. The transplantation of the Orthodox from Europe during the twentieth century did not lead to an outburst of creativity, and it is therefore unlikely that the American-born Orthodox of today and tomorrow will be able to do that much better.

The vast majority of affiliated Jews are currently members of Conservative or Reform congregations, and small numbers are identified with the Reconstructionist movement. While many among the leadership and the active members insist that major differences exist among these branches, the more striking finding is the steady narrowing of such differences, at least among the membership that falls within the central distribution of their respective movements. The overwhelming majority of congregants do not observe the Sabbath or follow the dietary laws; their children receive a limited Jewish education, which leaves most of them unable to read Hebrew, and they remain poorly informed about the Jewish past. Israel, however, represents an important center of their identification, and their rabbi officiates at critical ceremonies in their life-cycles — at circumcision, confirmation, marriage, death.

The major movements, Conservative and Reform, have built and maintained seminaries for the training of rabbis, but these institutions have not been able to maintain faculties of unquestioned distinction after the heavy pre-World War I inflow of scholars from Eastern and Western Europe came to an end and after the refugee professors from Germany and Austria in the 1930s had made their way to this country. In fact, the weakening of the seminaries as centers of Jewish learning is the other side of the successful expansion of Judaic studies at secular institutions of higher learning. While we took account earlier of this unexpected and large-scale expansion, it warrants further attention in the present context, since we are exploring here the potential for a vitalization of Judaism in the United States in the decades that lie ahead.

It is hard to see how the cultivation of Jewish studies can be anything other than positive. An expanded number of desirable and prestigious career opportunities are being opened up for scholars whose fields of specialization are one or another aspect of Judaica: Bible, literature, history, Talmud, philosophy, Holocaust studies. However, most colleges and universities appoint one or at most two faculty members to their Judaic department, which is not a critical mass for effective scholarly interchanges and is too few to support a graduate program leading to an advanced degree. But we are still in the early stages of this new receptivity of academe toward Judaica and it will take time before we can reach valid judgments about its stability, depth, and potential. At this early point in its evolution, Judaic studies at U.S. colleges and universities reflect favorably on the potential of U.S. Jews to make ongoing contributions to their tradition.

One of the tests for a creative Jewish experience in the United States would be a substantial improvement in the quality of books and magazines addressed to the best secularly educated community in the history of the Jewish people. Few would challenge the statement that the current output of popular and semi-scholarly articles and books is not impressive or that American Jews have never had a number of quality publications that seriously addressed issues of Jewish moment and attracted a broad-based authorship or readership. It is true that the economics of magazine publishing and book distribution presents increasing hurdles to accomplishing such goals, but a vibrant Jewish community requires that a significant minority of its members takes an active part in writing, reading, and debating critical issues that will shape its future. A passive community cannot be a creative community.

The third problematic force relates to the rapidly changing role of women in Jewish life in the United States. It is too early to assess their potential and future contributions, but the recent initial steps to broaden their scope for participation are a favorable augury.

The greater participation of women in synagogal services is still at an early stage, but the potential impact of that opening on their daughters and granddaughters will be considerably greater. In turn, the acceptance by both the Reform and the Conservative movements of women as rabbinical students will lead to a major addition to the leadership ranks. The seminaries have begun to appoint women to their faculties, a move that provides further reinforcement.

Admittedly this restructuring of tradition to enable women to become full participants in all aspects of Jewish life, not only within but outside the home, has carried the price of further estrangement between the mainliners and the Orthodox as well as precipitating new tensions within the Conservative movement. It is possible that the Conservative movement will at some time in the future splinter with the right wing, for whom the Halachah is authority, joining the Orthodox while those in the middle and left will align themselves with Reform to establish what would then be a much enlarged mainstream.

The foregoing is just one of several ways in which the women's revolution may alter significantly the structure and functioning of Judaism in America. What is less problematic is that a potential doubling of the pool of leaders is likely to have a great number of creative consequences for American Jewry, the nature of which cannot at this time be discerned.

Finally, the centrality of Israel must be entered into any equation that seeks to delineate the path of development for Judaism in the United States. The fact that the fate and fortune of Israel are difficult to foresee, even in broad outline, adds an element of uncertainty about the future shape of Judaism in the United States. Israel confronts a host of difficult problems domestically and in its external relations, for which it must seek answers even if the answers are at the moment elusive.

There is little prospect that the type of relationship American Jews have maintained with Israel during its first four decades, in which they raised large sums and transferred them to the Israeli leadership to be spent as the latter saw fit, will continue to be the pattern in the decades ahead. If Israel and the Diaspora are linked in indissoluble bonds as they have been throughout Jewish history, then it follows that each must have a deepened understanding and tolerance for the problems of the other. The conflicts that arose in the early 1970s about which should be the country of settlement for Jewish emigrants from the USSR; the opposition of many U.S. Jews to the war in Lebanon; the active intervention of the Conservative and Reform leadership with the Israeli government with respect to pending legislation to alter the criteria used to determine who is a Jew; and the mounting restiveness of many U.S. Jews with the excesses of the ultra-religious, ultra-nationalistic right—all are potent reminders that the American Diaspora will not long remain a passive partner in this ongoing relationship.

But if one postulates that creativity is linked to challenges, then the increasing pressure on American Jews to think and act on the problems they are encountering within the context not only of the changing U.S. scene, but also of their relationship to Israel, will present challenges that will stretch them. And in this stretching American Jewry may demonstrate new strengths that will lead to new achievements.

We are now at the end, an end that did not take shape until each of the foregoing chapters was in place. It is an end that in many respects is different from the assessment I had reached in my *Agenda*, where I saw only weakness and decline for American Jewry resulting from lessened respect and regard for religious tradition and legal precepts. Almost four decades later, I am by no means certain that American Jewry will have a flourishing future. But I am impressed by the potential of the four powerful forces that were hidden from my view in the immediate post-World War II years, the four forces that have been singled out for inspection in the preceding pages: the growth of neo-Orthodoxy; the proliferation of Jewish studies in Jewish day schools and in colleges and universities; the potential inherent in the new role for women in the American Jewish community; and the active participation of many American Jews in strengthening the state of Israel and the reinforced impact of that relationship on their own futures and the future of their children.

Each of the foregoing has a dynamism of its own that cannot be easily deflected or weakened. In sum it attests to the presence of strong creative forces. American Jewry is surely not doomed to go the way of Alexandrian Jewry, which over a relatively short time lost the creativity exemplified by Philo and disintegrated until the community totally disappeared. If the environment in the United States and in the world beyond remains reasonably supportive, with the world economy able to expand while peace is preserved, then the outlook for a creative Judaism in the United States must be judged to be favorable.

Selected Bibliography

American Jewish Yearbook. Vol. 88. American Jewish Committee and Jewish Publication Society. Philadelphia, 1988.

Arendt, Hannah. *The Jew as Pariah: Jewish Identity and Politics in the Modern Age*. New York: Grove Press, 1978.

Bell, Daniel. "Where Are We?" *Moment*, May 1986.

Bellow, Saul. *To Jerusalem and Back: A Personal Account*. New York: Viking Press, 1976.

Ben-Gurion, David. *Israel: A Personal History*. New York: Funk & Wagnalls, 1971.

Blitzer, Wolf. *Between Washington and Jerusalem*. New York: Oxford University Press, 1985.

Chafets, Ze'ev. *Members of the Tribe: On the Road in Jewish America*. New York: Bantam Books, 1988.

Chiel, Arthur A., ed. *Perspectives on Jews and Judaism: Essays in Honor of Wolfe Kelman*. New York: Rabbinical Assembly, 1978.

Cohen, Steven M. *American Modernity and Jewish Identity*. New York: Tavistock, 1983.

Cowan, Paul and Rachel. *Mixed Blessings*. Garden City, N.Y.: Doubleday, 1987.

Curtis, Michael, ed. *Anti-Semitism in the Contemporary World*. Boulder, Colo.: Westview, 1986.

Davidowicz, Lucy S. *On Equal Terms: Jews in America, 1881–1981*. New York: Holt, Rinehart & Winston, 1982.

de Lange, Nicholas. *Judaism*. London: Oxford University Press, 1986.

Dinar, Ben Zion. *Israel and the Diaspora*. Philadelphia: Jewish Publication Society, 1969.

Elazar, Daniel J. *Community and Polity: The Organizational Dynamics of American Jewry*. Philadelphia: Jewish Publication Society, 1976. Rev. ed., 1980.

Ellman, Yisrael. "Intermarriage in the United States: A Comparative

Study of Jews and Other Ethnic and Religious Groups," *Jewish Social Studies* 49, no. 1, Winter 1987.

Fein, Leonard. *Where Are We?* New York: Harper & Row, 1988.

Feldstein, Stanley and Lawrence Costello. *The Ordeal of Assimilation.* New York: Doubleday/Anchor Books, 1974.

Finkelstein, Louis, ed. *The Jews.* 2 vols., 3rd ed. New York: Harper & Row, 1960.

Friedman, Philip. *Roads to Extinction: Essays on the Holocaust.* Philadelphia: Conference on Jewish Social Studies and Jewish Publication Society, 1980.

Ginzberg, Eli. *Agenda for American Jews.* New York: Columbia University Press, 1950.

_____. *American Jews: The Building of a Voluntary Community.* In Hebrew. Tel Aviv: Schocken Books, 1979.

_____. *Keeper of the Law: Louis Ginzberg.* Philadelphia: Jewish Publication Society, 1966.

_____. *Report on American Jews: On Overseas Relief, Palestine and Refugees in the U.S.* New York: Harper & Row, 1942.

Glatzer, Nahum N., ed. *Modern Jewish Thought.* New York: Schocken Books, 1977.

Glazer, Nathan. *American Judaism.* Rev. ed. Chicago: University of Chicago Press, 1972.

Goldscheider, Calvin and Alan S. Zuckerman. *The Transformation of the Jews.* Chicago: University of Chicago Press, 1984.

Halkin, Hillel. *Letters to an American Jewish Friend.* Philadelphia: Jewish Publication Society, 1977.

Halperin, Samuel. *The Political World of American Zionism.* Detroit: Wayne University Press, 1961.

Harkabi, Yehoshafat. *Israel's Fateful Hour.* New York: Harper & Row, 1988.

Higham, John. *Send These to Me: Immigrants in Urban America.* Rev. ed. Baltimore: Johns Hopkins Press, 1984.

Johnson, Paul. *A History of the Jews.* New York: Harper & Row, 1987.

Kaplan, Mordecai M. *Judaism as a Civilization: Toward a Reconstruction of American Jewish Life.* New York: Macmillan, 1934.

Karp, Abraham J. *Haven and Home: A History of the Jews in America.* New York: Schocken Books, 1985.

Kaufman, Jonathon. *Broken Alliance: The Turbulent Times Between Blacks and Jews in America.* New York: Scribners, 1988.

Kop, Yaakov, ed. *Changing Social Policy: Israel 1985-86.* Jerusalem: Center for Social Policy Studies, 1986.

Lewis, Bernard. *Semites and Anti-Semites.* New York: W. W. Norton, 1986.

Liebman, Charles S. *Deceptive Images: Toward a Redefinition of American Judaism.* New Brunswick, N.J.: Transaction Publishers, 1988.

Lieberson, Stanley. *A Piece of the Pie: Blacks and White Immigrants since 1880*. Berkeley: University of California Press, 1980.

Lurie, Harry L. *A Heritage Affirmed: The Jewish Federation Movement in America*. Philadelphia: Jewish Publication Society, 1961.

Nathan, Robert R.; Oscar Gass; and Daniel Creamer. *Palestine: Problem and Promise*. Washington, D.C.: Public Affairs Press, 1946.

Oz, Amos. *The Black Box*. San Diego: Harcourt, Brace, Jovanovich, 1987.

Prager, Dennis, and Joseph Telershkin. *Why the Jews?* New York: Simon & Schuster, 1983.

Quandt, William B. *Camp David*. Washington: The Brookings Institution, 1986.

Roskies, David G. *Against the Apocalypse*. Cambridge, Mass.: Harvard University Press, 1984.

Rothchild, Sylvia. *A Special Legacy: An Oral History of Soviet Jewish Emigrés in the United States*. New York: Simon & Schuster, 1985.

Sartre, Jean-Paul. *Anti-Semite and Jew*. New York: Schocken Books, 1948.

Schwarz, Leo W. *Memories of My People*. Philadelphia: Jewish Publication Society, 1960.

Schweitzer, Avram. *Israel: The Changing National Agenda*. Dover, N.H.: Croom Helm, 1986.

Segre, Vittorio. *A Crisis of Identity: Israel and Zionism*. London: Oxford University Press, 1980.

———. *Israel: A Society in Transition*. London: Oxford University Press, 1971.

Shokeid, Moshe. *Children of Circumstances — Israeli Emigrants in New York*. Ithaca: Cornell University Press, 1988.

Silberman, Charles E. *A Certain People: American Jews and Their Lives Today*. New York: Summit Books, 1985.

Simons, Howard. *Jewish Times: Voices of the American Jewish Experience*. Boston: Houghton Mifflin, 1988.

Sklare, Marshall. *American Jews*. New York: Random House, 1971.

Soloveitchik, Joseph B. *Halachic Man*. Philadelphia: Jewish Publication Society, 1984.

Spiegel, Steven L. *The Other Arab-Israel Conflict*. Chicago: University of Chicago Press, 1985.

Tivnan, Edward. *The Lobby, Jewish Political Power and American Foreign Policy*. New York: Touchstone, Simon & Schuster, 1988.

Waxman, Chaim I. *America's Jews in Transition*. Philadelphia: Temple University Press, 1983.

Wyman, David J. *The Abandonment of the Jews*. New York: Pantheon Books, 1984.

Yerushalmi, Yosef H. *Zakhor: Jewish History and Jewish Memory*. Seattle: University of Washington Press, 1982.

Index

Jarvis, Samuel P., 61
Jaspers, Karl, 55, 61
"Jeckes," origin of term, 50
Jellinek, Georg, 54–55
Jellinek, Walter, 54
Jerusalem, 122–23, 147, 155
Jewish: affiliation, 150, 151, 164;
community, 18, 26, 28, 88–104, 153, 163;
education, 4, 11, 12, 14, 108, 141–43,
155–56, 164, 167, 168; identity, 49–50,
150, 152; immigrants, 105–9, 114, 121,
123; issues as topic for economists and
lawyers, 73; heritage thinning out, 88–
89, 91; history, 6, 12, 26, 89, 121, 123,
165, 166; law, 24, 150, 163–64, 168;
philanthropy, 10–11, 44; population in
U.S., 91, 111; religious ceremonies, 28–
30; scientists in U.S., 77–78; wealth and
U.S. universities, 44. *See also* American
Jews; Israel; Jewish day schools; Jewish
defense organizations; Jewish experience
Jewish Agency, 9, 75, 126, 143, 144; critics
of, 98
Jewish day schools, 142, 151, 167
Jewish defense organizations, 13, 46, 88,
100, 101, 157
Jewish experience, 140; and change, 12; in
the Diaspora, 1, 121–22; erosion in, 155–
57; in the U.S., 13, 18, 28, 139–52, 155–
62, 168–69. *See also* Anti-Semitism
Jewish Life in America (Rosen), 107
Jewish Occupational Council, 5
Jewish organizations. *See* Federations;
Jewish defense organizations; names of
individual organizations
Jewish "quotes" in U.S. higher education,
33
"Jewish Studies in the Universities," 143
Jewish Theological Seminary (JTS), 11, 12,
17, 18, 19, 20, 22, 57, 92, 94–95; women
in, 148
Jewish Thoreau, 121
Jewish Welfare Board, women in, 147, 148
"Jews in the American Economy: The
Dynamics of Opportunity" (Ginzberg),
107–9
Jews in higher education institutions, 33–
47
Jews, The (Finkelstein), 102
John XXIII, Pope, 14
Johnson, Charles, 115
Johnson presidency, changes during, 81–82
Johnson, President Lyndon B., 81, 82, 119
Joint Distribution Committee, 9, 75, 95, 97
Jordan, 135
Josephtal, Goria, 127

Judaic studies: in the seminaries, 169;
undertaking of, 154; in U.S. universities,
142–43, 152, 168
Judaism: American form of, 27, 166–67;
creative, 166, 170; essence of, 166; future
of, in U.S., 19, 20, 149, 151, 154–56,
166–70; new rationale for, 25; women's
revolution and, 169
Judaism (journal), 143
Judaism (Moore), 27
Judische Wissenschaft, 50

Kaplan, Annette, 42
Kaplan, Eliezar, 74, 126
Kaplan, Mordecai M., 25, 29, 151
Katie, 59
Keeper of the Law: Louis Ginzberg
(Ginzberg, Eli), 4
Keeser Lake, Maine, 106
Keezer, Dexter, 68
Kennedy, John F., 15, 82, 112
Kennedy-Johnson era, 82
Kibbutzim, 123, 127
Killian, James, 77
Kirk, Grayson, 40, 41
Kirk, Norman, 73
Kissinger, Henry, 82–83, 84
Kistiakowski, George, 77
Klutznick, Philip, 84
Knesset, 135–36; Arabs in the, 135
Knight, Charles, 66
Kohl, Chancellor Helmut, 161
Kollek, Teddy, 122, 125, 136
Krim, Arthur, 42
Ku Klux Klan, 106
Kupat Holim, 129
Kuznets, Simon, 107
Kyoto, Japan, 62

Labor Leader, The (Ginzberg), 63
Lake Messalonskee, Maine, 28
Landes, David, 39
Lazare, Bernard, 61
Leadership, American Jewish, 2, 9, 88, 96,
99, 105, 132, 140, 149, 156, 163; Israel
as, 26, 102–3, 145, 151–52, 161, 169–70;
lack of distinct, 95, 102; problems of,
102
Lederer, Emil, 54
Lenard, Phillip, 56
Lenin, Vladimir Ilich, 51
Lerner, Abba, 130
Levy, Gustav, 10
Lewis, Sinclair, 55
Lewy, Paul, 51
Lieberman, Mrs. Saul, 40